I0159945

QUAKERS, SOCIAL WORK, AND JUSTICE CONCERNS

Quakers and the Disciplines:
Volume 7

Edited by:
Max L. Carter
Erin Johnson
Jennifer M. Buck
Daniel Rhodes

Series Editor:
Paul Anderson

A Friends Association for Higher Education Book

i

Quakers
and the
Disciplines

Full Media Services
http://www.fullmediaservices.com

Friends Association for Higher Education
http://www.quakerfahe.org

Volume 1
Quaker Perspectives in Higher Education
May 2014

Volume 2
Befriending Truth: Quaker Perspectives
June 2015

Volume 3
Quakers and Literature
June 2016

Volume 4
Quakers, Business, and Industry
June 2017

Volume 5
Quakers, Politics, and Economics
June 2018

Volume 6
Quakers, Creation Care, and Sustainability
June 2019

Volume 7
Quakers, Social Work, and Justice Concerns
June 2020

Longmeadow, MA | Philadelphia, PA | Windsor, CT

Copyright © 2020
All rights reserved.
ISBN: 1-7336152-5-9
ISBN-13: 978-1-7336152-5-9

As a venture of the Friends Association for Higher Education, the Quakers and the Disciplines series gathers collections of essays featuring the contributions of Quakers to one or more of the academic disciplines. Noting historic values embraced within the Religious Society of Friends regarding particular fields of inquiry, each volume includes essays highlighting contributions by Quakers as means of addressing the needs of contemporary society. Each volume is designed to be serviceable within classroom and other discussion settings, fostering explorations of how pressing issues of the day might be addressed with creativity and passionate concern, informed by a rich heritage of faith, discovery, and action.

CONTENTS

LIST OF CONTRIBUTORS

Christy Randazzo is a scholar and activist whose work has been engaged in bridging the divide between the contemplative nature of theological writing with the active, lived theology of congregational life. They earned a PhD in Quaker theology from the University of Birmingham. They have published widely on Quaker constructive and reconciliation theology, Liberal Quaker history, peacemaking, political theology, and ecotheology. Their most recent publication is *Liberal Quaker Reconciliation Theology: A Constructive Approach* (Brill, 2020) They are a member of Haddonfield Monthly Meeting in Haddonfield, New Jersey, and currently teach at Montclair State University (New Jersey).

Daniel Rhodes is currently the undergraduate director of the Social Work program at UNC-Greensboro. Daniel received his PhD in Educational Leadership with a graduate certificate in Women and Gender Studies from the University of North Carolina at Greensboro in 2008. He received his Master's of Social Work from UNC-Chapel Hill in 1996 and has been a Licensed Clinical Social Worker (LCSW) in the State of North Carolina since 1999. Before coming to the Social Work department at UNC-Greensboro, Daniel taught in the Justice and Policy Department at Guilford College for four years; teaching a variety of course in the Community and Justice Studies major, including Conflict Resolution, Restorative Justice, and Community Building. Daniel also collaborated with the Peace and Conflict Studies major at Guilford College and co-taught courses in that major.

Daniel has 20 years of community-based, social work experience, working in community mental health, therapeutic foster care, serving as an AmeriCorp member working with immigrants and refugees and has been a clinical supervisor. He continues to work with immigrant and refugee populations in the area, specifically with immigrant Buddhist populations. Daniel also has a strong interest in issues of globalization and international social work and has traveled to Southeast Asia, as well as India, China, Palestine and Israel.

Doug Bennett (B.A. Haverford, PhD Yale) is President Emeritus of Earlham College where he served from 1997-2011. He taught political philosophy and public policy at Temple University, Reed College, Earlham College and now at Midcoast Senior College in Maine. He is a member of Durham Friends Meeting in New England Yearly Meeting. He is currently at work on preparing *A Faith and Practice for Quaker Organizations*.

Jennifer M. Buck is an Assistant Professor of Practical Theology at Azusa Pacific University. She holds a PhD in Philosophy of Religion and Theology from Claremont Graduate University and an MDiv from Fuller Theology Seminary. She is a licensed minister in the Evangelical Friends church and serves on the pastoral staff of Northland Village Church in Pasadena, CA. She is the author of *Reframing the House: Constructive Feminist Global Ecclesiology for the Western Evangelical Church* (Pickwick, 2016) and of two forthcoming books: *Distinct: Quaker Holiness in Everyday Life* (Barclay Press) and *Bad and Boujee: Towards a Trap Feminist Theology* (Fortress Press).

Linda B. Selleck is a retired Friends minister and educator. She holds a B.M.E. degree in Music Education and Piano from Greensboro College, North Carolina and a M.A. in Church History from the Earlham School of Religion in Richmond, Indiana. A native of Southampton County, Virginia, she served Friends in Indiana, Illinois, Pennsylvania, Ohio, North Carolina, and Jamaica. Linda has taught music at all grade levels and has performed hundreds of programs as a sacred Celtic harpist. Her book, *Gentle Invaders: Quaker Women Educators and Racial Issues During the Civil War and Reconstruction*, was published in 1995 by Friends United Press. Linda and her husband Ron now live in Sioux Falls, South Dakota where they enjoy their children and grandchildren every day.

Mark Bredin (PhD, St Andrews University) is a Quaker who until recently was a managing chaplain in prison. He now works as a hospital chaplain. He has published various books/articles relating to non-violence, the ecological crisis, people with learning difficulties, chaplaincy, and the poor in Matthew's Gospel. He has taught at St. Andrews and Cambridge University and St. Philips Theological College in Tanzania. He lives in King's Lynn, UK, with his wife Fran, daughter Hannah and granddaughter Maddie. He is writing a book on Lucretia Mott and the Bible.

Max L. Carter taught in Friends secondary schools in Ramallah and Philadelphia and at Earlham College and Guilford College, retiring in 2015 from Guilford as the William R. Rogers Director of Friends Center and Quaker Studies. His 1989 PhD dissertation at Temple University was on Quaker relations with Midwestern Indians in the early 1800s. His most recent book is *Palestine and Israel: A Personal Encounter* (Barclay Press, 2020).

Nelson Bingham has been a faculty member in Psychology at Earlham College since 1974 and is currently Emeritus Professor. A convinced Friend, he is a member of West Richmond Monthly Meeting (part of the New Association of Friends). He has been a member of the Friends Association for Higher Education since 1982, serving on the Executive Committee, as Co-Clerk, and on the Nominating Committee. In 2001, he participated in a study tour of Quaker sites in England with the Earlham School of Religion faculty and staff, including a visit to The Retreat at York, which allowed for observations, interviews and gathering materials that form the basis for this article.

Paul N. Anderson serves as Professor of Biblical and Quaker Studies at George Fox University in Newberg, Oregon and as Extraordinary Professor of Religion at the North-West University of Potchefstroom, South Africa. Author or editor of fifteen books, and publisher of that many more, some of his noted books include *The Christology of the Fourth Gospel; The Fourth Gospel and the Quest for Jesus; From Crisis to Christ; and Following Jesus: The Heart of Faith and Practice.* Paul served as editor of *Evangelical Friend* and *Quaker Religious Thought,* and in addition to editing the Quakers and the Disciplines Series (FAHE), he is editor of the Biblical Interpretation Series (E. J. Brill) and the Johannine Monograph Series (Wipf & Stock).

Wendy Grab MSW/LISW is the Assistant Professor of Social Work for Wilmington College. She has also taught for the Master of Social Work programs at both Tulane University and Miami University and has a passion for multicultural social work and has lived, worked, studied, and volunteered abroad. She has worked with several multicultural groups, including urban Appalachians, Hispanic Americans, refugees, immigrants, Native Americans, and in Scotland with heroin addiction.

Wendy studied at Antioch College, majoring in a self-designed undergraduate degree in Art Therapy and received her Master's Degree in Social Work from the University of Kentucky. She has practice experience with many different populations, including at risk families, mentally ill adults, foster children/families, developmentally delayed adults, heroin addiction, support groups, and high school students/families. In addition, Wendy is a Health RHYTHMS facilitator, exploring the effectiveness of this program with college student challenges such as stress, anxiety and depression.

Introduction

In this volume of the Friends Association for Higher Education's series on Friends and the academic disciplines, ten authors apply theory and history of Quaker work for social change in offering insight into how Friends have approached social work.

This collection of essays is divided into three sections. The first considers theory of social work and change. Christy Randazzo applies the work of John Paul Lederach to a theological understanding of Quaker testimony and social action. Daniel Rhodes shares about his application of Quaker principles in his educational work with social work students. Douglas Bennett describes the history and development of Quaker organizations in addressing social issues.

A second section looks at individual Quakers' lives and their work. Paul Anderson examines the life of prison reformer Elizabeth Fry, Mark Bredin discusses progressive reformer Lucretia Mott, and Wendy Grab considers the Quaker influences on social work pioneer Jane Addams.

The third section considers collective work of Friends in addressing social issues. Nelson Bingham explores the creation of the first mental hospital, the York Retreat, begun by Friends in England. Max L. Carter describes the work of Friends among Midwestern Indians in the early 1800s. Linda Selleck draws from her book *Gentle Invaders* to share the history of Quaker women's educational work among African Americans before and after the Civil War. Jennifer Buck details Quaker involvement in the women's Suffrage movement.

1| The Place of Testimony: Quaker Testimony as Reconciliation Framework

By Christy Randazzo

This chapter argues for a new way of imagining Quaker testimony and theology, particularly relating to the role of truth in peacemaking, through placing Quaker testimony in dialogue with the "place of reconciliation" framework for peacemaking developed by John Paul Lederach.

In his seminal work on peacemaking, *Building Peace*, Lederach first explicated his vision of reconciliation as a "place" both literal and metaphorical where humans can give space for others to engage in the praxis of healing society after conflict (Lederach, 1997). This "place of reconciliation" is the meeting point between truth, mercy, justice, and peace, where each is understood conceptually (as values foundational for society, equal in merit and necessity for peacemaking) and praxeological (attendant processes and instruments flowing from the conceptual foundations, such as Truth Commissions and criminal trials, for example). This framework has been instrumental in the development of post-conflict theologies of reconciliation and atonement, particularly due to its dialogical balancing of concept and praxis, which holds both ontology and ethics as equally valuable in peacemaking.

This chapter affirms that this concern for balancing theology and ethics strongly reflects Quaker theologies of interdependence and testimony. Quaker interdependence theology is expressed metaphorically, where the metaphor of Light expresses the Quaker experience of "an immanent God who is concomitantly connected to all of creation", who is therefore also equally present in each individual Quaker (Randazzo, 2019, p. 102). As the Divine is interdependent upon, and interconnected with, humanity, humanity is called upon to acknowledge, and respond, to the interconnection. Quakers term this response "testimony" because it entails speaking the truth about the human condition. Quakers view testimony as a form of faithful witness, where they interpret the work of the Spirit and the Spirit's call for humanity to live into the truth of that work (Muers, 2015). Quaker testimony is therefore multifaceted, lying at the intersections of theology and ethics, and the individual and the community, encompassing all at the same time. The Quaker conception of testimony is generally seen as a holistic reflection of the Quaker community's core theological beliefs and ethical convictions, where Quaker interpretation of these beliefs and convictions is embodied, and expressed, in the actions of Quakers (Muers, 2015). Reflecting a well-known Christian hymn based on John 13:35, therefore, Quakers are known by their actions, in that to be a Quaker is to live Quaker testimony through one's entire being: to act "Quakerly" is both ill-defined, yet also immediately understood by Quakers as the goal of Quaker life.[1]

While testimony is therefore a holistic totalizing of Quaker meaning, it has traditionally been broken down into discrete elements over time, with a "testimony" to peace being the most consistent over time. Testimony lists serve the purpose of making concrete and specific the ambiguous, and all-consuming, concept of "Quakerliness"; thus, they can serve as effective pedagogical and evangelical tools, allowing Quakers to teach others about the core doctrinal elements of a tradition known for its insistent rejection of dogmatism and specificity. These lists have often closely reflected their cultural and historical context, in that they are inherently open to revision and reconsideration as Quakers are forced to respond to changing times and situations (Mendl, 1974).

Viewing testimony through the lens of Lederach's quadrant, with its sense that the core goal of reconciliation necessitates the balancing of four core elements, therefore opens creative avenues for re-imagining Quaker conceptions of testimony. I propose a reframing of Quaker testimony such that a core of Quaker testimony is reconciliation, with attendant "testimonies" which reflect ways Quakers have framed traditionally framed testimony (truth, equality, peace), and one way which I claim is inherent within Quaker testimony (mercy). I first provide a brief definitional background to both reconciliation as a secular and theological construct as well as to Lederach's quadrant theory. I explore the concept of "embodied peacemaking" through the dual lenses of Quaker testimony and virtue theory, offering a framework for bringing Quaker testimony and Lederach's reconciliation quadrant into dialogue. I argue that a reconciliatory Quaker virtue testimony would consist of the four elements discussed above. I provide a brief introduction to Quaker definitions of these concepts, and offer suggestions for developing these concepts further, both in terms of Quaker theology and in line with Lederach's thought.

---

1   John 13:35, NRSV: "By this everyone will know that you are my disciples, if you have love for one another."

Reconciliation as Secular and Theological Construct

Practitioners and academics in the fields of reconciliation and conflict transformation seek insights from other traditions and perspectives in order to move the conversation of peace beyond the debate between pacifism and just war. Reconciliation theology is one of the recent examples of this trend. Reconciliation theology seeks to determine what the reconciled human-human, and human-divine, relationship would actually look like and be achieved. This relationship is exemplified in the "Kingdom of God" preached by Jesus Christ. Reconciliation is thus not interested in violence, per se, but more with the effort to heal the community after violence, in all of its forms, has harmed the community. Reconciliation works on four levels: the theological, between God and humans; the interpersonal, between individual people; the social, between local, alienated communities; and the political, across an entire nation or region. Each level carries its unique complexities, yet are all sequential processes with different goals for each sequence (de Gruchy, 2002).

In the political realm, reconciliation is also known as conflict transformation. Simon Fisher, in describing a Quaker approach to conflict transformation, defines it as a "holistic and multi-faceted process", which is directly accountable to those most affected by the conflict. It is also buttressed by a network of organizations, government agencies, local leaders, and individual actors who all work towards the goal of bringing positive change to behaviors, attitudes, structures, and relationships (Fisher, 2004, p. 27).

Conflict transformation also views violence from a holistic perspective, where violence can be both visible and invisible, physical as well as structural (Fisher, 2004). Physical violence is thus simply the visible manifestation of a deep undercurrent of invisible violence in the form of structural discrimination, poverty, and oppressive systems whose source can be located in negative attitudes such as hatred, racism, and intolerance. Conflict is not inherently negative nor violent, however. Rather, conflict occurs in human relations and often precipitates creative problem-solving (Tutu, 2000).

Fisher (2004) views conflict as a basic incompatibility between behaviors and goals. When the behavior and goals of actors are incompatible, open conflict ensues; when either the behaviors or goals are incompatible, the conflict is a surface, or latent conflict. Conflict management is thus a balance between a concern for maintaining or healing relationships with others alongside a concern for achieving the goals of the actor or organization. Different approaches can thus result from the different concerns of the people involved (Mendl, 1974).

Conflict transformation seeks a broader change, analyzing the roots of the conflict with the goal of an eventual transformative reconciliation that might stem the tide of further conflict (Fisher, 2004).

This multi-faceted approach comes from the inherently complex nature of conflict itself, and the complicated web of structures, relationships, and history that creates and sustains conflict (Lederach, 2005). This view is not shared by all actors and organizations involved in conflict transformation, however; some seek to impose a 'one-size-fits-all' approach to conflict (Kistner, 2003). This approach is viewed dimly by Fisher. He stresses the necessity for conflict transformation to be approached humbly, with an awareness of prejudices and assumptions that could lead actors to impose their own perceptions on the conflict. They should instead approach their work from a place of creativity, flexibility, and with an awareness of the multiple levels of the conflict (Fisher, 2004).

Reconciliation is thus a totalizing process, touching on every single aspect of a society. John De Gruchy (2002) argues that this process requires a shift from contractual relationships between members of society to covenantal relationships, where all are mutually interdependent. Humble acceptance of guilt, apology for harm caused, and forgiveness all must occur in order for any rebuilding of trust and renewed relationship, and thus reconciliation, to occur. These covenant relationships thus require a culture rooted in common practices, values, and a recognition of God's role in covenant building (Everett, 1999).

The Place of Reconciliation

In *Building Peace*, John Paul Lederach (1997) develops a framework for imagining protracted, systemic conflict as an interconnected web of relationships and interactions between people, institutions, identities, and ideologies within which humans are bound. Lederach stresses that one is incapable of comprehending a conflict by focusing on specific elements of the conflict, such as either the institutional elements, or specific actors. Only by examining the conflict as a whole, and attempting to discern the relationships between the parts at play in the conflict, can any sense be made of the conflict itself (Lederach, 1997). Reconciliation is therefore relational, in that it focuses on addressing the relationships between the elements in a system of conflict, whether those relationships exist between elements at the macro level of ideology and ethnicity, the mezzo level of political institutions, or even the micro level of individual actors. By focusing on relationship, one can see the web of connections between the different levels or elements of conflict which might remain obscured by a focus on one specific level or element. In this way, it can be said that Lederach (2005) views reconciliation as "places" where these varying elements can encounter each other.

Lederach leans on Jewish imagery of peacemaking through a creative re-appropriation of Psalm 85:10 to develop what he terms "the quadrant of reconciliation". While participating in a meeting of local peacemakers during the war between the Contras and the FSLN (Sandinista National Front) in Nicaragua during the 1980's, Lederach (1997) heard someone read Psalm 85:10, which in the translation he heard states "Truth and Mercy have met together; peace and justice have kissed" (p. 28). The phrase was apparently common enough in this setting that Lederach heard it regularly during similar meetings across Nicaragua, leading him to see in it a powerful metaphorical framework for understanding reconciliation as the "place" where the values – and attendant practices – of truth, mercy, peace, and justice meet. The intertwined concepts of meeting and "place" extend throughout Lederach's imagery of reconciliation, as both metaphorical conceptions and as literal meetings between people in actual, geographical places (Lederach, 1997, p. 27).

Lederach (1997) recognizes that these four elements can often be in conflict with each other, so this place of encounter is inherently dynamic, always seeking to fund harmony amongst contradictory elements. It is precisely these contradictions which give scope and meaning to the elements, however. Lederach viewed the elements as being joined: Truth with Mercy, Justice with Peace. Truth is acknowledging harm and validating experiences of loss and pain, while Mercy involves acceptance, forgiveness, and the release of the past with the intent of seeking a new beginning. Justice is a search for rights, social restructuring, and restitution from harms done, while Peace emphasizes the need for interdependence, security, and health (Lederach, 1997). The elements are interdependent, and balance each other, blunting their worst impulses while having the potential to bring each element to fruition in powerful and unexpected ways.

David Stevens (2004) elucidates ways which this process plays out by exploring the relationships between each of the four elements, demonstrating that, for example, justice and truth involve both accountability and acknowledgement, where one must have the acknowledgement of truth in order to then have the attendant accountability of justice. Stevens underlines the importance of balance in these relationships, however, stating that while truth cannot ignore justice by simply acknowledging a wrong without demanding accountability, justice cannot simply sidestep truth by imposing accountability that outstrips the weight and severity of the acknowledged wrong. The elements are therefore not buttons to be pushed, where one can simply impose a one-size-fits-all justice, but rather dynamic forces which must be continually assessed and adapted to ensure that they remain in balance (Stevens, 2004).

It should be noted at this point that while Lederach provides broad definitional outlines of each of these elements, he keeps the specifics of the quadrant deliberately vague. This reflects the overall emphasis in reconciliation theory on remaining open to the context of the conflict, and on being willing to adjust the response to the context. Lederach (2005) suggests that each individual reconciler should engage in a 'moral imagination', where the reconciler views the practice of reconciliation as an art, stemming from deep personal immersion in the values of reconciliation. For example, Truth could involve the very specific processes of a Truth Commission, a war crimes tribunal, public apologies, any combination of these, or even something else entirely. The main focus of reconciliation is to create the "space for encounter" amongst all parties in the conflict, where the parties can abandon a cognitive focus on issues and instead embrace an innovative approach to addressing the relationships bound within the "place" of conflict (Lederach, 1997, p. 35).

The practice and ethos of reconciliation are not separable for the individual reconciler. This reflects Lederach's understanding of reconciliation as both a *focus* and a *locus,* in that reconciliation is a perspective focused towards the human relational element of conflict as well as a phenomenon of space, where those in conflict encounter each other (Lederach, 1997). In this sense, therefore, "reconciliation" serves as both a holistic, "reconciliatory" way of being which informs every aspect of the reconciliation process and the humans engaged in that process, as well as a practical approach to healing relationships between institutions, ethnicities, and people post-conflict.

Stevens uses the language of virtue to explain this "way of reconciliation", stating that the attitudes, habits, and practices of reconciliation actually form a set of reconciliatory virtues which are necessary in order to spread reconciliation throughout an entire society (Stevens, 2004, p. 37). Stevens suggests a long list of virtues, yet insists that rather than each specific virtue being requisite, that they reflect an overall reconciliatory approach to being and acting. Any virtue can work, as long as it serves the main focus of reconciliation. These virtues are not simply known, as if they were simply cognitive processes one could rationally follow, step-by-step. Instead, Stevens (2004) asserts that the virtues must be experienced in relationship, with people who embody the virtue in their entire being. In this way, these virtues are communal, experienced in the intimate places of personal relationships, and in the physical places of schools, churches, and social institutions. These virtues must be nourished and taught in all places of a person's life, such that a person becomes themselves a place of reconciliation:

they embody reconciliation to the extent that every place they exist becomes a place of reconciliation due to their presence in that place.

Quaker Testimony as Embodied Reconciliation:
A Virtue Theory of Testimony

From a Quaker perspective, embodying reconciliation sounds remarkably similar to the language of testimony, specifically as it relates to peace. Testimony amongst the Early Quakers was an embodied reflection of the "Light of Christ" within the person, and the ethical life which resulted from the alignment of the individual's will with the will of God (Gwyn, 2006, p. 114). The practical expression of this testimony involved any number of ethical and moral norms, including behavior and outward appearance; yet, the norms were still understood to be aspects of an overall testimony of the person's alignment with the will of God for the building up of the eschatological "Kingdom of God".

A Quaker is therefore one whose character is entirely shaped by their testimony to the will of God active within the person (Dale, 2007). As Roger Wilson (1949) argues, while Quaker ethics rests on the teachings of Jesus which emphasize a responsibility to demonstrate care for all persons in their actions, Quakerism is not foundationally a service organization. Instead, Wilson places worship of God as the primary responsibility for Quakers. Wilson stresses that worship of God will open their hearts to both God's all-consuming love for all of creation, and to the need to express that love in compassionate action. Wilson insists that this experience is not simply an individual call, meant to be held tight, and silent, by the individual Quaker. As worship is both communal and individual, the individual ethical call must be presented to the community of the Quaker meeting to determine if this was a call to the community to engage in similar work. This call is also tested against the gathered wisdom of the broader Quaker 'testimony' that has developed both within that community, and in the wider community of Quakers (Wilson, 1949). If the call is borne out through this entire process, Wilson argues, it is incorporated into Quaker 'testimony; that is, the complex structure of 'being Quakerly'.

Liberal Quaker thought has taken the concept of the 'testimony' of a Quaker's life rooted in the worship of God, and developed from that overall 'testimony' a typology of specific ethical norms, termed "testimonies", within which the overall Quaker ethical framework could be placed. This has led to the proclamation of a variety of Quaker testimonies, across the spectrum of Quaker expression, often reflecting the theological and ethical concerns of the specific Quaker community developing the list. Jonathan Dale (2007) has termed this a difference between 'broad' and 'particular' testimonies. 'Particular' testimonies might develop which provide greater specificity and definition to Quaker ethical thought; however, they are simply specific applications deriving from the broader Quaker testimonies of social care, peace, and the Light of God within each person.

Tim Newell (2000) suggests that the testimonies of equality, community, simplicity, stewardship, and integrity all fit within a tight ethical framework, where each testimony builds upon the others and depends for its meaning on the other testimonies. Removing any one 'testimony', or even ignoring the call to embody that testimony, would destroy the entire ethical framework upon which the Quaker understanding of the necessary human response to God's love rests. Newell does not give much structure to these testimonies, nor any specific, defined requirements that the testimonies demand beyond providing examples of how Quakers can embody the testimonies in the general pursuit of justice: the focus of Newell's reflections on the Quaker response to the criminal justice system. In this, Newell demonstrates a distinctly Quaker approach to ethics: developing ethical responses, in light of Quaker testimony, from within a very specific context.

The concept of an embodied Quaker testimony of reconciliation can answer those who critique the Liberal Quaker typology of 'testimonies'. For one, Rachel Muers (2007) notes that the concept of 'particular' testimonies has transformed from an ethical framework to, at least in popular Quaker thought, a list of rules limiting Quaker behavior. These rules might concur in practice with the overall Quaker testimony that Wilson advocates, yet stem from a different ethical and epistemological foundation. John Punshon (1990) notes that the values that Quakers espouse in their testimony structure do not vary in any significant outward way from the secular values of many in what he terms 'the counterculture'. Punshon (1990) argues that these overlaps with 'secular' ethical structures allow many people to feel a sense of common cause with Quaker action, without having to ever accept the spiritual, and for many, Christian, foundation of the Quaker testimony.

In order for rules to have any weight, they must stem from a proscribed set of norms that are applicable to all people, and whose outlines can be specifically delineated. In other words, any expression of the 'testimonies' as rules, or even as normative proscriptions on Quaker behavior, actually betrays the existence of a defined set of beliefs about the necessary ethical response to the creation against which a person's behavior can be judged. This sounds suspiciously like a creed, something which Liberal Quakerism in particular has made a significant point of rejecting. In light of this, Quaker ethical thought, especially regarding peacemaking, should be structured along a framework that allows for the fluidity of response to the context that reconciliation theory demands, such as that found within the realm of virtue theory.

This is not unique to Quakerism. In his work on political reconciliation, Daniel Philpott (2012) argues that as political reconciliation is inherently contextual, and pursues the rather vaguely outlined values of forgiveness, healing, mercy, and justice, the most proper ethical framework would be virtue ethics. Philpott develops a communal model of virtue that he calls an 'overlapping consensus', where multiple perspectives on reconciliation all come to a consensus about the definition and outline of reconciliation, due to overlapping similarities in the philosophical, ethical, and religious perspectives on peacemaking and reconciliation of each person involved. Philpott (2012) argues that as this overlapping consensus grows, it is increasingly affirmed in the society, and is thus more likely to succeed. Thus, an ethic that can build consensus around common values, such as virtue ethics, is more likely to lead to a society which affirms the value of reconciliation. Philpott specifically calls for religious communities to be active in this work, as, he contends, they would be most likely to have the most effective ethical resources upon which to build such a consensus.

Quaker ethical consideration has already begun to incorporate the language of virtue theory, with Jackie Scully as the most prominent thinker developing these ideas. Scully (2008) has suggested that the typology of testimonies limits the concept of testimony to that of moral and ethical guides divorced from an underlying theological construct for the Quaker life. Scully argues that Liberal Quakerism should thus develop a vision of the testimonies as constituent virtues rooted in an overarching testimony of love for "that of God" within each person, of which peace would be seen as the practical outgrowth (p. 116). Echoing Newell's perspective on the role of the peace testimony, Scully (2013) notes that Quaker ethical consideration around issues of peacemaking is a complex weave of testimonies, or values, where each constituent value depends on the others in order to make any sense in the overarching Quaker ethical structure. Thus, the testimony to peace is incomplete without an awareness that conflict is rooted in inequality, corruption, and the materialism, all of which intersect with the testimony to equality, integrity, and simplicity.

Scully's work notes areas where virtue theory and Quaker ethics do not entirely overlap, especially as virtues are the dispositions of a "good life", while the testimony is the reflection of a faithful life. This allows for what Scully (2008,) terms a "deontological tether" to exist in Quaker ethical thought: a generally virtue-based ethical structure which is nonetheless shaped by the deontological call to recognise 'that of God in everyone' (p. 121). This creates an ethical collage where each virtue testimony is actually aspects of one core virtue testimony: that of "Quakerliness", shaped by the injunction to seek God within the other, which can often be illuminated by the experience of worship. From a Quaker perspective, therefore, those who engage in reconciliation as Lederach frames it can thus be said to embody reconciliation as a virtue, or a testimony. The Testimony of reconciliation is a "place" where the testimonies of Truth, Mercy, Justice, and Peace meet.

Quaker Virtue Testimonies of Reconciliation

For Quakers, the definition of each of these virtue testimonies is presented as generally accepted in the abstract, yet becomes exponentially more complex as one attempts to develop a framework for its boundaries (i.e. answering the question of what Truth is, and is not), and to then determine how to apply it to one's daily life in the form of specific practices. Of course, this could be due to the fact that the meaning of each of these concepts cannot be removed from the context which provides structure to that meaning, as continental philosophy, feminist philosophy, and Quaker philosopher Grace Jantzen argue (Jantzen, 1998). While acknowledging the inherent challenge in providing a universal definition of Truth which could then be easily translated into specific practices which would apply to all people, this is not actually the intent of Quakers when they develop a testimony framework, whether that be Truth, Peace, Equality, or Mercy.

Instead, before simply declaring the existence of a testimony which applies to the entire community, Quakers are cautious about engaging in the creative reimagining of Quaker testimony on one's own, removed from conversation with the wider Quaker community (Punshon, 1990). The development of new frameworks of testimony is a process which is necessarily complex, as it involves a dialogue between those who seek to speak prophetically to the conscience of the entire community and those who are listening to the voice of the Divine to determine if this new direction is a faithful response to that voice (Punshon, 1990). This process takes significant deliberation and care, must be rooted in a strong sense of religious conviction and spiritual truth, and reflect communal discernment. Thus, testimonies arise from the experience of Quakers, reflecting on the Divine will in community, who seek to determine the direction that Quaker Testimony more broadly is, and should be, taking. This is a form of "experimental learning", where Quakers seek to continually reflect on their experiences to determine what values and habits of being – which Quakers previously felt reflected their experience – are still useful and can be inhabited in their current, and specific context (Muers, 2015).

While certain testimonies have generally stood the test of time and continue to speak to Quaker experience of Testimony – such as the virtue testimonies listed here – they are all open to the same process of continuing revelation which Quaker theological and ethical concepts are held to: as God is continually speaking, Quakers must be continually open to new revelations about where their Testimony is to move towards, and how it is to develop. This ensures that Quaker ethics can be flexible enough to continuously have meaning for Quakers throughout time, while also be specific enough to respond to actual circumstances (Muers, 2015). Thus, the concept of a testimony to Peace, for example, can be flexible enough to be applied in one way towards the threat of state oppression during the reign of Charles II in the seventeenth century, while retaining both its historical meaning for Friends as well as its nimble applicability when applied to the complexities of asymmetrical non-state terrorism.

It is with this perspective in mind that I present brief outlines of these four virtue testimonies as constituent elements of an overarching Quaker reconciliation virtue testimony. I provide a brief definition of these terms, as they are currently understood amongst Friends, and then offer a framework for imagining them elements of a wider web of reconciliation theology and ethics.

Truth

The testimony to truth relies on a multi-faceted definition of the concept of truth, ranging from being honest in one's individual dealings with others, through aligning one's life to a teaching accepted as "true" (such as peacemaking), all the way to proclaiming the Divine as "Truth", what Dale terms "the nature of God, which is pure integrity" (Dale, 2007, p. 85). This reflects the intertwining of action and theology inherent in Quaker testimony, where the ethical frameworks of honesty which Quakers have long emphasised as integral to a Quakerly approach to engaging with others is rooted in, and reflects, an understanding of the Divine as the one who is Truth itself. Truth is therefore dependable, and can be relied upon to reveal what is "true", where "truth" is understood as that which is both foundational to the world, and necessary for maintaining the harmony and balance of the good order of creation. To live "truthfully" is to both always be honest in one's dealings with others as well as to align oneself with the essence of Truth, which is the will of the Divine for the creation, as well as the essence of the Divine Being itself (Young Friends General Meeting, 1988, p. 82).

Reflecting ethics, Quakers are called to "speaks truth" in one's speech or actions as the Divine is itself Truth, a Truth which calls upon us to live lives reflecting the presence of the Divine within (Punshon, 1990). Reflecting theology, the presence of the Divine Truth within means that Truth is both universal and particular: universal because the Divine Truth is present in the entire creation, particular because individual humans experience the Truth of the Divine presence in vastly divergent ways which nonetheless are all experienced as "truth". These various experiences of Truth are not simply "glimpses of truth", pieces of the Divine which neatly fit alongside each other in a composite mosaic of "Divine Truth" (Ullman, 1961, p. 52). Instead each individual's experience of the Divine Truth is paradoxically both the entirety of Truth (as the Divine cannot be divided into human-sized pieces), and only a partial, particular expression of the Divine (as interpreted through the individual's particular hermeneutical constructs) (Wildwood, 1999).

This paradox of particular and universal applies to the "truth" of peacemaking. Fisher stresses that Quaker embrace of the particular entails accepting multiple truths, and multiple experiences of truth, allowing them to all exist alongside each other without demanding that they be shaped to conform to a universal narrative of "truth", especially in situations of trauma and conflict (Fisher, 2004, p. 63). Yet, underlying all truths is the universal truth of a Divine present in all. This "truth" of the unity of the creation requires a human witness to the truth of unity, and the practices of peacemaking which are necessary to witness to unity.

Peace

Quakers have long felt a call to peacemaking, marking it as one of their central tenets (Steven, 2005). Termed 'the peace testimony', Quakers have based much of their reconciliation and conflict transformation work on the strength of this idea (Hubbard, 1991). This testimony is itself rooted in the concept of divine inter-relationality with every individual human (Braun, 1950). Quakers term this construct the 'Light Within', and it has both a theological aspect and an ethical one: if each person is in relationship with God, then each person's life is sacred and must be treated with respect (Hodgkin, 1916). Quaker testimony on peace is also rooted in the love that God feels for every single person, making violence against other humans in some sense a violence against God. An interesting result of these two interlaced concepts is that if violence against one person is violence against God, and if all people are in an interdependent relationship through God, then violence against one person is somehow violence against all people. Peace-building is therefore an essential practice for Quakers, for the selfish reason of self-preservation (Lacey, 2010). Quakers are very well aware of the dangers of total war.

Yet, peacebuilding is so central to Quaker ethical thought because it is seen as the fullest expression of the embodiment of the Quaker testimony of worshipping a God who loves the entire creation. Quakerism could this be said to have an incarnational vision of peace, where Jesus as incarnate God demonstrates the fullness of God's love for the creation, with Quakers called to embody of testimony of active following in Christ's example (Lonsdale, 1953). Quakers are called to live peace in their lives, in every aspect of their lives. Adam Curle (1981) thus argues that the peace testimony is severely limited if it only applied to questions of physical or state violence. Curle contends that peace must be a human condition, which is fostered in every aspect of a person's life. For Curle, peace is a condition that must be embodied in everyday human interactions in order to become so rooted in a person's character that it can shine through in their pursuits of peacebuilding on a broader scale (Curle, 1981). In this, Quakers could be said to agree with Lederach's argument that reconcilers must embody reconciliation in their person, in order to bring reconciliation to their specific context by means of the reconciler 'being reconciliation' itself. John W. Harvey (1921) agrees, and goes on to make an explicit connection between peacebuilding and reconciliation, arguing that the two concepts are actually integrally linked and thus inseparable. Reflecting this, and Simon Fisher's expansive definition of conflict transformation, I think that a more complete understanding of the Quaker testimony to peace must include a testimony to reconciliation. Thus, any Quaker ethic of peace is also an ethic of reconciliation, and can productively be placed in dialogue with reconciliation theory and ethics.

Equality

Similar to Mercy, Quakers have not delineated a specific testimony to Justice, yet much of the same elements which constitute Justice (redressing imbalances, the search for rights, social restructuring, and restitution from harms done) reside within the traditional framework of the testimony to equality. As with all of the previous virtue testimonies explored here, equality stems from the fundamental Quaker theological tenet that the Divine is present within all. Equality emerges from a logical extension of this: as the Divine is universally present throughout creation, that necessarily implies that the Divine is universally present within particular persons, all particular persons are brought in unity through the Divine present in each and every one of them (Randazzo, 2020). The action of Divine love both flattens, and makes sacred, the particularities of each person. The love of God is complete, whole, and unified, and as such, individual persons are all equally loved by the Divine presence in creation (Randazzo, 2019). However, as God shows love through the act of creation, this inevitably includes each individual person, meaning that God is not just present within the particular, but the love of God is inherently for particular persons as unique individuals.

Reflecting Quaker testimony, therefore, Quakers are called to show the love of God for others by not only ensuring that all people are equally free from oppression, injustice, war and violence, and poverty, but are given space and the actual, physical resources they need to grow into the unique gifts given them by God both for bringing into being the Divine will, but also for human enjoyment. The way that Quakers frame the testimony to equality aligns with the way that Lederach frames justice, in that imbalances between people, the lack of equal access to – and respect for – the rights of marginalized groups, and the need to offer restitution for injuries and loss to people and communities are all issues of equality, and the pursuit of both justice and equality will inevitably lead to re-envisioning both the structures which undergird society and the relationships which bind and give form to human communities. Quakers have devoted significant attention to developing the outlines of the testimony to equality, such that Quaker discussions of equality are always issues of justice, whether it be racism (McDaniel and Julye, 2009), gender equality (Quaker Women's Group, 1986), economic injustice (Harvey, 1942), amongst countless other examples, or the absolutely innumerable ways that Quakers have examined issues of violence from the perspective of equality. Quakers view equality as the lens through which to frame questions of justice, and explain their particular approach to achieving justice through the methods they have developed to achieve equality across humanity.

Mercy

There has not been, to this point, an explicit testimony to mercy or compassion delineated in any of the extant testimony lists, yet it lies at the foundation of Quaker peacemaking work specifically, and Quaker work for social change more generally. As with the other testimonies described here, a Quaker testimony to mercy rests on the foundation of the fundamental unity of all of creation through the presence of the Divine within all people, which renders sacred all human life (Brain, 1944). What makes a testimony to mercy unique is a specific focus on recognizing humans as individual beings which experience pain and suffering, and on a divine call to relieve that suffering both due to compassion for that individual person's suffering, and an empathetic recognition that the unity of all people through the Divine presence means that we can only live fully into our humanity when we open ourselves to the suffering of others (Hodgkin, 1916).

This is intensely personal – and intimate – work, and demands a willingness to be uncomfortably, and even dangerously vulnerable to others to a far greater extent than any of the three other testimonies described above. Mercy cracks us open emotionally, and lays us bare to the emotions of others. This includes every aspect of humanity, whether they be the unpleasant parts (unfortunate personality traits, for example), or even the potentially dangerous ones, such as cruelty and malice (Lampen, 1987). Yet, this also means that we are fully open to experiencing, and sharing in, the joy and love of other humans. This level of intimacy means that we aren't only experiencing the overwhelming love of God for the creation, we are also experiencing the beautiful, messy, and intimate love of particular people, in specific circumstances, and appreciate it all the more because it is real, tempered by challenge and hardship, and deepened by time (Hoare, 1946). These are true relationships, made all the more complete by the experience of struggle. It is precisely this relationship of respect and love for others which Scully argues is the "starting point and beacon for ethical navigation" (Scully, 2002, p. 82). Love for the other is thus the heart and soul of a testimony to mercy, and thus the starting point for a Quaker virtue testimony of reconciliation.

Conclusion

This chapter explored the "place of reconciliation" framework for peacemaking developed by John Paul Lederach, through the lenses of virtue theory and Quaker testimony. I developed a new way of conceptualizing Quaker testimony and theology, a "virtue testimony of reconciliation", where I imagined what reading the overarching concept of Quaker testimony through the framework of reconciliation would look like. This involved a brief overview of Lederach's theories, including an exploration of the concept of reconciliation in both Lederach's work and in the work of Quaker reconciliation practitioners. As the reconciliation quadrant involves examining the relationship between the particular practices/concepts of justice, peace, mercy, and truth with the broad practice/concept of reconciliation, I proposed a framework of a general testimony of reconciliation resting upon four particular testimonies – truth, equality, peace, and mercy. Three of the testimonies (truth, equality, and peace) are recognized within the tradition as reflecting long-standing conceptualizations of Quaker testimony, whereas I argued that while mercy was not recognized as a specific testimony to date, it underlay traditional Quaker testimony frameworks, and was thus a valid expression of testimony.

I based my testimony framework on extant Quaker testimony language, while simultaneously shifting the focus of the language to reflect a core testimony of reconciliation, where reconciliation is "embodied" both in the person as a "place of reconciliation", and in the reconciliatory actions of the person. The concept of embodied testimony reflects the concerns for character development inherent in virtue theory, and also reflects Lederach's insistence that reconcilers must be embedded in peacebuilding contexts in order to be the most effective at their work.

My framework of testimony is dependent upon Jackie Scully's exploration of Quaker testimony as a virtue ethic. Scully's work has only begun to scratch the surface of the connections between testimony and virtue theory. I believe that Quakerism can provide a unique contribution to such an overlapping consensus of virtue ethics, especially as relating to reconciliation ethics and practice as the Quaker testimony of reconciliation provides a robust and complex ethical construct for peacemaking. Much more work needs to be done on these points of intersection; yet, I believe that a fruitful dialogue between Quaker ethical thought on peacemaking and reconciliation and conflict transformation/reconciliation theorists would benefit both communities.

Discussion Questions

1. In what ways would this application of Lederach's reconciliation quadrant theory to Quaker ethics and theology challenge, and complement, traditional Quaker definitions of testimony? Do these challenges, and complements, reflect your own experience with, and understanding of, the ways that testimony is defined, and works within Quaker frameworks?

2. How does the concept of "embodied testimony", with its particular focus on the connections between virtue theory and Quaker embodied ethics, intersect with Lederach's focus on embodied peacemaking? Do you find Randazzo's argument persuasive? Why or whynot?

3. The author argues for the inclusion of a new testimony in the traditional Quaker testimony framework - mercy - and by extension, argues for a more fluid and flexible understanding of the ways which Quakers adopt new testimonies. Does this argument challenge Quaker understandings of testimony? How so?

References

Brain, W. R. (1944). *Man, society, and religion.* The Swarthmore Press, Ltd.

Braun, K. (1950). *Justice and the law of love.* George Allen & Unwin, Ltd.

Curle, A. (1981). *True justice: Quaker peace makers and peace making.* Quaker Home Service.

Dale, J. (2007). *Faith in action, Quaker social testimony.* E. Cave and R. Marley (Eds.). Quaker Home Service.

de Gruchy, J. W. (2002). *Reconciliation: Restoring justice.* Fortress Press.

Everett, W. J. (1999). Going public, building covenants: Linking the TRC to theology and the church. In J. Cochrane, J. de Gruchy, and S. Martin (Eds.), *Facing the truth: South African faith communities and the Truth and Reconciliation Commission.* Ohio University Press.

Fisher, S. (2004). *Spirited living: Waging conflict, building peace.* Quaker Books.

Gwyn, D. (2006). *The covenant crucified: Quakers and the rise of Capitalism.* Quaker Books.

Harvey, M. M. (1942). *The law of liberty.* George Allen & Unwin, Ltd.

Harvey, T. E. (1921). *The long pilgrimage: Human progress in the light of the Christian hope.* Robert Davis.

Hodgkin, H. T. (1916). *The missionary spirit and the present opportunity.* The Swarthmore Press, Ltd.

Hubbard, Geoffrey. (1991). *Patterns and examples: Quaker attitudes and European opportunities.* Quaker Home Service.

Jantzen, G. M. (1998). *Becoming divine: Towards a feminist philosophy of religion.* Manchester University Press.

Kistner, U. (2003). *Commissioning and contesting post-apartheid's human rights: HIV/AIDS, racism, truth and reconciliation.* Lit Verlag.

Lacey, P. (2010). *The unequal world we inhabit: Quaker response to terrorism and fundamentalism.* Quaker Books.

Lampen, J. (1987). *Mending hurts.* Quaker Home Service.

Lederach, J. P. (1997). *Building peace: Sustainable reconciliation in divided societies.* United States Institute of Peace Press.

Lederach, J. P. (2005). *The moral imagination: The art and soul of building peace.* Oxford University Press.

Lonsdale, K. (1953). *Removing the causes of war.* The Swarthmore Press, Ltd.

McDaniel, D. and Julye, V. (2009). *Fit for freedom, not for friendship: Quakers, African Americans, and the myth of racial justice.* Quaker Press of Friends General Conference.

Mendl, W. (1974). *Prophets and reconcilers: Reflections on the Quaker Peace Testimony.* Friends Home Service.

Muers, R. (2007). "It is worse to be evil than to do evil": Dietrich Bonhoeffer's challenge to the Quaker conscience. In J. L. Scully & P. Dandelion (Eds.), *Good and evil: Quaker perspectives.* (pp. 173-182). Ashgate Publishing Limited.

Muers, R. (2015). *Testimony: Quakerism and theological ethics.* SCM Press.

Newell, T (2000). *Forgiving justice: A Quaker vision for criminal justice.* Quaker Books.

Philpott, D. (2012). *Just and unjust peace: An ethic of political reconciliation.* Oxford University Press.

Punshon, J. (1990). *Testimony and tradition: Some aspects of Quaker spirituality.* Quaker Home Service.

Quaker Women's Group. (1986). *Bringing the invisible into the light: Some Quaker feminists speak of their experience.* Quaker Books.

Randazzo, C. (2019). "The divine light of creation": Liberal Quaker metaphors of divine/creation interdependence. In C. Bock and S. Pothoff (Eds.), *Quakers, creation care, and sustainability* (Vol. 7 in the Quakers and the Disciplines Series). Full Media Services.

Randazzo, C. (2020). *A Quaker ecotheology of light.* Brill Publishing.

Scully, J. L. (2002). *Playing in the presence: Genetics, ethics and spirituality.* Quaker Books.

Scully, J. L. (2008). Virtuous friends: Morality and Quaker identity. In P. Dandelion and P.Collins (eds), *The Quaker Condition: The Sociology of a Liberal Religion* (pp. 107-123). Cambridge Scholars Publishing.

Scully, J. L. (2013). Quakers and ethics. *The Oxford handbook of Quaker studies.* Oxford University Press.

Steven, H. (2005). *No extraordinary power: Prayer, stillness and activism.* Quaker Books.

Stevens, D. (2004). *The land of unlikeness: Explorations into reconciliation.* The Columba Press.

Tutu, D. (2000). *No future without forgiveness.* Image Books.

Ullmann, Richard. (1961). *Tolerance and the intolerable.* George Allen & Unwin, Ltd.

Wildwood, Alex. (1999). *A faith to call our own: Quaker tradition in the light of contemporary movements of the Spirit.* Quaker Home Service.

Wilson, R. C. (1949). *Authority, leadership and concern.* The Swarthmore Press, Ltd.

Young Friends General Meeting. (1998). *Who do we think we are?: Young Friends' commitment and belonging.* Quaker Home Service.

2| The Landscape of Quaker Organizations

By Doug Bennett

When American Quakers encounter a need or a problem, a most common response is to create an organization to deal with the matter – a Quaker organization. Creating purposeful organizations to deal with problems and to improve the world is something Quakers have been doing abundantly since the 17th century.[1]

Over the past two centuries, American Quakers have created more than a dozen institutions of higher education, scores of k-12 schools, a network of retirement homes, several retreat centers, many summer camps, and an array of service agencies and advocacy organizations. These organizations constitute one of the principal contributions of the Religious Society of Friends in this country. Bear in mind that there are fewer than 100,000 Quakers in the U.S. today.[2]

The array of Friends Schools is perhaps most impressive. Friends Council on Education draws together Quaker Schools and other Quaker organizations with a mission in education. Among its members today are about 80 Quaker schools that serve children up to high school graduation. Three of these

---

[1] For helpful and corrective comments on earlier drafts the author is grateful to Max Carter, Thomas Hamm, and those who attended the session where this was first presented at the 2019 gathering of Friends Association of Higher Education.

[2] Mark Myers, who has served on the board of many Quaker organizations, provided this rough accounting in 2012:

"[We] have been very successful in the creation and expansion of Quaker-related organizations that serve our body and the society around us. Examination of U.S. Quakerism today finds 80 Friends schools, 18 colleges and universities, 22 retirement communities, 8 retreat study centers and over 70 organizations for Quaker service, publishing, health care, peace advocacy, and lobbying and other social action undertakings. One can easily count this number to a level of over two hundred organizations and not include standing committees within the 32 yearly meetings." (Myers, 2012).

schools trace their founding to the 1600s: Friends Select (1689) and William Penn Charter (1689), which share a common founding, and Abington Friends (1697). Eleven were founded in the 1700s, and fourteen in the 1800s. The impulse to create new Friends Schools continues: at least six FCE member schools have been founded since 2000.

We are still creating Quaker organizations. Generally they arise from a strongly felt moral purpose, a 'leading,' Quakers say. Abolition of slavery, equal educational opportunity for girls and boys, prison reform, humane care for the mentally ill, climate justice, retirement living with dignity: these and dozens of other purposes have drawn the attentions of Quakers over decades.

The organizations Quakers have created command the respect of both Friends and non-Friends. Presidents Clinton and Obama chose to send their daughters to Sidwell Friends School in Washington, D.C., for example. The American Friends Service Committee and the British Friends Service Council accepted the 1947 Nobel Peace Prize for Quaker work on relief and reconstruction during and after World War II. Quaker organizations are frequently singled out by those who work in peer non-Quaker organizations as models in terms of their service excellence, effectiveness in the use of resources, moral clarity and integrity.

Of course, other religious denominations also create organizations. There are Episcopalian schools, Methodist and Presbyterian colleges, Christian Science reading rooms and a newspaper, Roman Catholic schools and colleges and hospitals and so on. Relative to our numbers, however, Quakers have created an unusually large number of organizations. There is meaningful substance to the Quaker identity of these organizations. To know that an organization is Quaker is to have some assurance of its quality. It is also an assurance that the organization will function as a community, that it will act with integrity, and that it will place a high value on equality in its programs and activities.

Asked what makes an organization Quaker, those who know Quaker organizations will often point to their use of consensus in making decisions, to their highly egalitarian or participatory cultures, to their emphasis on respect for all persons, to their preference for informality, or to their high concern for integrity in all phases of their functioning. These and other characteristics seem fiercely important to those who work in or are served by Quaker organizations. These characteristics arise straightforwardly from the faith and practice of Friends.

At the same time, among Quakers there is a discomfort with their organizations — especially with their larger or more successful ones. To many

Friends, the very idea of formal organization suggests wealth and power; Quakers are generally more comfortable confronting wealth and power than deploying them. There is a paradox here: an impulse to create organizations and at the same time a recoiling from supporting and sustaining these same organizations. Pick up a work of Quaker religious belief or practice. No matter which you choose, likely there will be hardly any mention of Quaker organizations. And yet many more people experience Quakerism through these organizations — the schools, colleges, camps, retirement homes and advocacy organization — than through Quaker Meetings or Churches.

Here I simply want to illuminate the organizational impulse among Friends and to identify a few of the pathways by which the array of Quaker organizations has come into being. At the end I will consider what makes an organization Quaker, a question that is contested ground.[3]

Worship Organizations Among Friends

The first Friends organizations were worship communities: Friends churches you might call them, but early Quakers were more given to call them Meetings. The local worship communities are called Monthly Meetings, because their members gather once each month to transact whatever business comes before them. Monthly Meetings group themselves into larger networks of Quarterly Meetings that meet four times a year to worship together and transact additional business, and Quarterly Meetings group themselves into Yearly Meetings that meet annually for worship and business. In early days of Friends, the ambit of Yearly Meetings was the area from which people could gather after no more than a day's travel.[4]

Monthly, Quarterly and Yearly Meetings do more than make arrangements for worship. They also provide pastoral care for their members. They provide for the religious education of children, they make arrangements for marriage and death, and they make arrangements for care of the sick and troubled.

---

[3] This paper is part of a larger project on Quaker organizations. The central aim of the project is to compile *A Faith and Practice for Quaker Organizations*. Every Yearly Meeting (a regional assembly of Quakers) has its own *Faith and Practice*, a compilation that describes Friends practices and beliefs. But these works are nearly silent about Quaker organizations. At best they name a few with which the Yearly Meeting has some affiliation and provide contact information. The say next to nothing about the religious underpinnings of these organizations or about how they should conduct themselves.

[4] Before 1900, Monthly Meetings usually embraced more than one congregation, each of which was called a preparative meeting.

Typically, various committees of the Meeting and on a mostly volunteer basis undertake these activities.[5]

Monthly Meetings, Quarterly Meetings, Yearly Meetings: this array was the original organizational fabric of American Quakers, and we still have it today. Call this the *worship fabric* of Quaker organizations.

This organizational array that makes up the worship fabric of Quaker organizations is quite old. Quakerism began to take shape in the early 1650s in England as groups of seekers, dissatisfied with the Church of England, the Roman Catholic Church and nascent protestant churches, coalesced around George Fox, an itinerant preacher. In 1652, Fox had a powerful epiphany on Pendle Hill in which he sensed that the Lord "had a great people to be gathered." Over the next dozen or more years the movement that came to be called Quaker drew together powerful numbers and energy and also was subjected to legal persecution. Fox himself went to jail. When he was released from imprisonment in September 1666, he was worried that the formlessness of the young Quaker sect could imperil its future. He set his mind and talents to give the inchoate movement some organizational shape. Margaret Fell joined him in this organizational work.

"During the next two years, he toured the length and breadth of England organizing a system of church government so strong and yet so resilient that it has lasted until the present time. Largely as a result of this intensive work, the whole fabric of the Society of Friends as it exists today was built up during his lifetime" (Vipont, 1954, p. 97). This account is from Elfrida Vipont, a distinguished historian of Quakerism. By "whole fabric," Vipont meant the organizational form of the Religious Society of Friends.[6] But there is more to the whole fabric than just these Monthly, Quarterly and Yearly Meetings.

There has never been a national denominational organization for U.S. Quakers. This is unusual among religious groups. In Quakerism, each Yearly Meeting is a realm unto itself. Today, there three umbrella organizations that group together similarly minded Yearly Meetings for some common purposes. Friends General Conference (FGC) serves a grouping of more theologically lib-

---

[5] In many Quaker Meetings, those present gather in silence and speak when they feel moved. There is no order of worship and no pastor. Such unprogrammed Meetings may have a paid secretary or coordinator if they have a large number of members. Other Friends Meetings have programmed worship and may employ a pastor.

[6] For a fuller account, see Arnold Lloyd (1950). Elton Trueblood (1966) has an appendix titled "Quaker Organization" that lays out this array of Quaker worship organizations, pp 285-287. Quakers in Britain today organize their worship somewhat differently: http://www.quaker.org.uk/our-organisation/our-structures.

eral Yearly Meetings in the United States and Canada that feature mostly unprogrammed worship. Friends United Meeting (FUM) serves a grouping of Christ-centered Yearly Meetings in North America and Africa, most of whom are pastoral. The Evangelical Friends Church International (EFCI) serves a grouping of evangelical, pastoral Yearly Meetings. There are also Yearly Meetings that describe themselves as Conservative (unprogrammed) and these do not have an alliance organization. Some Yearly Meetings are affiliated with both FGC and FUM, and there are unaffiliated Yearly and Monthly Meetings. Most (though not all) Yearly Meetings belong to Friends World Committee for Consultation (FWCC) whose purpose is to "encourage fellowship among all the branches of the Religious Society of Friends."

Testimonial Organizations Among Friends

Beyond the worship fabric of American Quakerism, and largely parallel to it, has arisen another array of organizations created and sustained for purposes other than religious worship and care of members. These are schools, colleges, retirement homes, service or advocacy organizations, camps, retreat centers and more.

We can and should see these organizations as arising from the worship life of Quakers. In worshipping together, Quakers come to feel *concerns* that all is not right with the world — that things should be made better, either just among Friends or more broadly. Those concerns ripen into *leadings* about how the situation might be improved. And those concerns and leadings, all arising in worship and therefore from one spirit, have formed a pattern of how Friends should engage the world. "Quakers have expected the Light of Christ to lead them in the same direction and toward the same goals. Because revelation is continuing, new leadings will come, but because Spirit is consistent, certain principles will prevail. Friends have called these principles 'testimonies' because they witness to the wider world of the power of God to transform individuals and human society" (Birkel, 2004, p.104). Today among Friends, these testimonies are often captured in the acronym SPICES: concerns with Simplicity, Peace, Integrity, Community, Equality and Stewardship of the earth.[7]

In some ways each individual can and should live out these testimonies personally, but some efforts require joining with others in coordinated effort — in organizations. The organizations that Quakers have founded beyond the worship fabric of organizations are ones created to pursue or enact these testimonies:

---

[7] The idea of 'testimonies' can be found in very early writings of Friends. The framing of these as SPICES is much more modern, often attributed to Howard Brinton (1943).

to provide a good education for both boys and girls, to work for peace and justice, to care for the elderly and so forth. Call these the *testimonial fabric* of Quaker organizations.[8]

There is considerable variety in the purposes, sizes and approaches of the testimonial organizations and the focus of organizational effort has changed over the centuries. Without any attempt at providing a proper history or even a fully inclusive accounting, what follows is a sketch of the emerging scope and range of Quaker organizations — a survey of the landscape.

Paths to the Creation of a Quaker Organization

Here is one account of the creation of a testimonial Quaker organization, Abington Friends School.

"In the spring of 1697, John Barnes, a member of Abington Monthly Meeting, donated 120 acres of his estate 'for and towards erecting a meetinghouse for Friends and toward the maintenance of a school under the direction of Friends" (Abington Friends School, n.d.).

In the beginning, the school occupied a single room in the meetinghouse; it took nearly a century for the school to have its own building. Today, more than 300 years after its founding, the school is still located on the grounds of Abington Friends Meeting and operates 'under the care of' that Meeting. It is the oldest school in the Commonwealth of Pennsylvania continually operating in the same location.

Abington Friends may be unusually old, but the pathway of its founding is quite common among Quaker schools. Many Quaker meetings came to operate schools, at least primary schools, for their own children, to give them a guarded education in the manner of Friends. These schools were often located in the Meetinghouse and governed under the care of the Monthly Meeting that had created them.

While it is common for a Quaker organization to be created by a Monthly or Quarterly Meeting, this is not always the case. Some Quaker organizations began as the initiative of a single individual. This second pattern of founding, as a proprietary organization, was more common a century and more

---

[8] At the end of his Appendix on "Quaker Organization" in *The People Called Quakers*, Elton Trueblood (1966) says simply this: "There are also a great number of auxiliary organizations such as the service organizations already described in chapter 13. Many of the organizations have come into being because of particular "concerns" felt by a few individuals. In Quaker language, "concern" is something about which someone feels so deeply that he is moved, almost against his will, to do something about it. Organizations which arise in this way are so numerous that they cannot be mentioned." For a more contemporary overview of Quakers in the World, see Thomas Hamm (2003), pp. 155-183.

ago before the creation of not-for-profit status in law. By way of example, this is how Sidwell Friends School recounts its founding:

"Thomas Watson Sidwell opened Friends' Select School (as Sidwell Friends was then known) in 1883 as an initiative in co-ed, urban day-school education. Sidwell, then 24 years old, had been a teacher at Baltimore Friends School, headed by the leading Quaker educator Eli Lamb. Lamb opened the way for Sidwell to begin a school in Washington by sponsoring authorization of the venture within the Baltimore Yearly Meeting. While the Alexandria Monthly and Baltimore Yearly Meetings offered some nominal assistance, the operation was a proprietary one from the beginning" (Sidwell Friends School, n.d.).

It was not until 1934 that Sidwell Friends was reorganized and incorporated as a nonprofit institution under a Board of Trustees.

Some Quaker organizations are created by groups of individuals in a manner deliberately independent of any Monthly or Yearly Meeting. In the 1830s, for example, Philadelphia Yearly Meeting could not reach unity on a proposal to create a Quaker college. A group of Quakers, members of Philadelphia Yearly Meeting, met separately and created a Corporation to found Haverford College. This third pathway to founding is exemplified by another Quaker organization, the Friends Historical Association which today publishes *Quaker History* and organizes annual gatherings of its members:

"On the evening of 12 mo. 4, 1873, nine Philadelphia Friends met at the home of Dr. S. Mason McCollin on the northwest corner of Fifth and Callowhill streets and took the first steps toward the formation of what was to become the Friends Historical Association. ... The nine Friends who were present approved the proposal and a committee was appointed 'to prepare a statement of the objects of the association and of the proposed plan of conducting the same" (Moore, 1974, p. 35).

At a second meeting a month later, a constitution was approved; officers were elected and committees appointed a month after that. From the very beginning the intention was to create an organization of substance and permanence. Those gathered at the first meetings made provision for a written mission statement, a constitution, legal incorporation, property holding, a governing board and committees, and regular meetings. Today these are features of many Quaker testimonial organizations no matter which their founding pathway.

Among the initiators of the Friends Historical Association were both Orthodox and Hicksite Friends (Hamm, 2003). "[T]hese nine men represented both branches: five of them were Arch Street Friends while four were members of the Race Street Yearly Meeting. When the permanent organization was effected, the original Board of Directors consisted of fourteen persons, and the two branches were equally represented" (Moore, 1974, p.35). Whatever divided the two branches at that time did not interfere with their common purpose in this instance, and those on both sides were comfortable in creating an organization.[9]

Many other such founding stories could be told. It is sufficient to note from these examples that not all Quaker organizations have been created in the same way: some have been created by individuals, others by groups; some have been created in close attachment to Monthly or Yearly Meetings, and many have been deliberately created with independence from organizations in the worship fabric of American Quakerism.

By and For Friends: Early Quaker Organizations in the United States
Schools

The earliest testimonial Quaker organizations were Quaker schools, first primary schools, later secondary schools as well. Many Monthly Meetings created Friends schools and sustained them 'under the care of the Meeting.' Concerted efforts were made to provide schools so that nearly every child of a Quaker family could receive at least a primary education in a Friends school. By 1750 there were about 60 Quaker schools under the care of one or another Monthly Meeting in Philadelphia Yearly Meeting alone and more than one hundred within that Yearly Meeting by the end of the century (Kenworthy, 1987). Many of these schools have passed from the scene, largely displaced by the rise of public education, but ten of these continue.

These earliest Quaker schools were created to provide "a guarded education" for Quaker children; they were, to use a different Quaker terminology, "select" schools. Creating schools that would allow their children to be educated within Quaker beliefs and practices was one strong impulse. Another was the concern that education be provided equally for girls and for boys. Admitting its first students in 1799, Westtown School is the oldest, continuously operating coeducational boarding school in the United States. In the early decades of the 19th century, Friends created an array of secondary schools, generally called academies, the majority of them boarding schools under the care of Quarterly or occasionally Yearly Meetings. In Indiana Yearly Meeting alone, there were two dozen such academies (McDaniel, 1939).

---

[9] The Friends Historical Society, a similar Quaker organization was created in 1904. The two were merged into one organization in 1923. FHS was the larger organization at that time, but FHA, with virtually no members, had a certificate of incorporation, so the newly merged organization proceeded as Friends Historical Association.

Colleges

With many colleges and universities first founded to educate the clergy of various denominations, and with Friends suspicious of 'hireling ministers,' Quakers were at first reluctant to create colleges and universities. In the 19th century, the desire to educate teachers for Friends schools in a Quaker setting was one concern that led to a turn to create colleges. Haverford College, founded in 1833, was the first. Earlham College began as the Friends Boarding School in 1847 and became Earlham College in 1859. The Baltimore Association of Friends of the Southern States provided assistance to New Garden Friends School (established 1837) allowing it to remain open despite the ravages of slavery and the Civil War, and to be transformed into Guilford College in 1880s. The other colleges Quakers have created were also founded later in the 19th century, especially in the 1870s and 1880s. Many of these were founded by or in conjunction with Yearly Meetings (Oliver & Charles et. al., 2007).

The schism that divided Quakers into Orthodox and Hicksite branches beginning in the 1820s led to the creation of further Quaker schools and colleges. Because many of the already-founded educational institutions remained with the Orthodox, Hicksites formed their own, such as Swarthmore College (1864) and George School (1887).

Publishers

Lacking a central or national denominational organization, Friends had difficulty printing and disseminating written materials. According to Edwin Bronner (1967), "Friends belonging to Philadelphia Yearly Meeting were receiving virtually no printed material from the yearly meeting in 1816" (p. 345). Moreover, "there was no periodical. Friends did publish some books, but it is clear that a minimum of Quaker printed material reached Friends homes" (Bronner, 1967, p. 345, n.11). Thus, it is not surprising that publishers were another kind of early Quaker testimonial organization.

The Tract Association of Friends (1816) was created in 1816 "for the printing and distributing of moral and religious books and pamphlets such as explain and enforce the doctrines of the Christian religion" (p. 346). It is still publishing. Friends Publishing Corporation is the successor organization (a complicated history) to *The Friend*, a publication for Quakers that began in 1827. Today, this organization publishes *Friends Journal* and also produces *QuakerSpeak* videos.

Schools and Publishers

These were organizations *within* the world of Friends. They were of, by and for Friends. Early Quakers in the United States provided charity or benevolence to one another when difficulties arose. This was accomplished largely through funds administered by Monthly, Quarterly and Yearly Meetings. Individual Friends might provide assistance to those who were not Friends, but through their early organizations, Friends generally looked only after their own. The good they might do others was to draw them into their understanding of Christianity. "By doing non-believers the supreme good, by drawing them to Truth, the early Friends knew that they would arrive at a state of affairs where no problems about charity to people of other persuasions would exist," (James, 1963, p.25-26) concludes Sydney James. "They saw their own immediate needs, though, and organized to aid each other systematically. They wanted to create a perfect circle and enlarge it" (James, 1963, p.25-26).

Prisons and Hospitals

Beyond the perfect circle, nineteenth century Quakers did take an interest in the treatment of the most troubled persons in society. In prisons, they pressed for the separation of men and women, something first implemented in the United States in Philadelphia's Walnut Street Jail (1790), and then pressed for separate cells for all prisoners — the penitentiary system, first implemented at the Western Pennsylvania Prison in Pittsburgh (1821) and the Eastern Pennsylvania Prison in Philadelphia (1829) (Quakers in the World, n.d.) These organizations were maintained by the state, of course; they were not Quaker organizations. Quakers also took an interest in the treatment of the mentally ill. Drawing on the British Quaker organization, The Retreat at York founded in 1792, American Quakers founded The Asylum for the Relief of Persons Deprived of the Use of Their Reason in 1813 to provide a humane alternative to the cruel way those with mental illnesses were treated at the time. It continues today as Friends Hospital (Price, 1988), (Cherry, 1989).

Beyond the Perfect Circle

By the middle of the 19th century, Friends schools and colleges had begun admitting those who were not Friends; they were no longer 'select schools.' When Germantown Friends School was established in 1845, there were Quakers and non-Quakers among its first students. Germantown Meeting was unsettled about this practice, however. Lacking enough Quaker students for solvency, the school opened and closed a few times before 1885 when a non-Friend was admitted.[10] It has remained open on this basis ever since.

At Earlham College, the first person who was not a Quaker was admitted in 1859, the year the school transitioned to becoming a college. A tuition surcharge for those who were not Quakers was eliminated in 1878, and the first faculty member who was not a Quaker was hired in the 1880s (Hamm, 1997). By the end of the 19th century, virtually all Friends schools and colleges were enrolling students who were not Friends — so long as they were White.[11]

Schools for African-Americans

Concerns with slavery and the challenges facing enslaved peoples were important in drawing Quakers towards providing service and assistance to others. There were some efforts to create Quaker schools to provide for the education of African-Americans, but with some exceptions these were kept separate from schools for Quaker children (Hamm, Beckman, Florio, Giles & Hopper, 2004). These were among the earliest Quaker organizations that reached beyond Friends. As early as 1750, Anthony Benezet established a school in his home "in which Quaker students were taught during the day and African American students were taught in the evening" (McDaniel & Julye, 2009, p.124). In 1837, a bequest from Quaker Richard Humphreys allowed founding of the Institute for Colored Youth to teach useful trades.[12] Friends in Philadelphia also founded Bethany Mission in the 1850s, a Sabbath day school (that is, holding classes only on Sunday) that lasted until the 1930s. Other Friends were involved in creating schools (many of them short-lived) that served African Americans in Virginia, Delaware, Maryland and Indiana (McDaniel & Julye, 2009).

In their Yearly Meetings in the decades leading up to the Civil War, Friends came to insist that there be no slave holding among them. Many individuals supported abolitionist organizations, but as numerous as Quakers were in these organizations, such organizations probably should not be considered Quaker ones. After the Civil War broke out, Friends struggled with the question of participation in war: many young Friends did serve. Most Yearly Meetings

---

[10] Germantown Friends School, Historical Highlights. https://www.germantownfriends.org/about-us/historical-highlights.

[11] On Earlham College's slow movement to admitting African-American students, see Bennett (2001). For Germantown Friends Schools halting progress towards admitting those not Quaker, and towards admitting African Americans, see its Historical Highlights on its website.

[12] In 1902 the Institute was relocated to George Cheyney's farm, to the west of Philadelphia. In 1983, the institution (whose name had changed several times) was taken into the State System of Higher Education as Cheyney University of Pennsylvania (Conyers, 1990).

had committees that raised money for purposes of relief as the war released many African Americans from the bonds of slavery and those released flooded into refugee camps.

Towards the end of the Civil War, and in the aftermath, Quakers worked with the newly established Freedmen's Bureau to establish schools for those now freed from slavery. "In many instances, the Freedmen's Bureau and Quakers opened a school together; at other times the Bureau asked individual Friends to start a school in a particular location or assume control of one it could no longer maintain" (McDaniel & Julye, 2009, p.154). Many of these were proprietary schools, most of them not lasting beyond the ministry of their founder.

By the end of the 1860s, Quakers were providing support to hundreds of such schools, though it is difficult to say how many of these might be considered Quaker schools. The most prominent of these organizations was Southland School in Arkansas, established by Quakers Calvin and Alida Clark in 1864. Southland became a college in 1869 when it established a normal school that trained teachers for many other schools. Southland College persisted until 1925 (Southland College, n.d.).

Schools for Native Americans

Quakers also established schools for Native American children. Though some were established earlier, Quakers (as well as other denominations) worked with the Grant administration between 1869 and 1877 in establishing a few dozen schools, some of them day schools but the majority of them boarding schools to "civilize and Christianize" Native American children. Most of these had a few dozen to perhaps a hundred students and were mostly located on Native American reservations in Kansas, Oklahoma and Nebraska. Quakers also administered schools for Native Americans in Alabama, North Carolina, Ohio, Iowa, Arizona and Alaska. The largest of these Quaker Native American Boarding schools was the Tunesassa Friends School for Seneca children that operated in Quaker Bridge, New York from 1852 to 1938 (Palmer, 2019).

Through the 18th and 19th century, Quakers and Quaker Meetings were involved in a range of additional reform issues. Individual Friends joined organizations created by others to advance causes such as temperance, prison reform and women's rights. But aside from the worship fabric of Monthly and Yearly Meetings and their associated the schools and colleges, Quakers created relatively few organizations of their own to advance these causes.

Missions

With the coming of missionary work, this began to change. In the latter half of the 19th century and impelled by a rising evangelical fervor that swept across the United States, Quakers engaged in missionary work often in league with other, especially Protestant, organizations. At first this work was undertaken by individual Friends who felt a strong leading. They were often coordinated by missionary efforts of British Friends. In time, a number of Yearly Meetings created Mission Boards to coordinate mission efforts of that Yearly Meeting.

In 1881, the Woman's Missionary Union of Friends in America (today, the United Society of Friends Women International) was created to provide a vehicle for Quaker women to support missionary work. In 1887 the American Friends Board of Missions was created to coordinate the mission work of eight Yearly Meetings, generally those in the Five Years Meeting, later Friends United Meeting. Other Yearly Meetings maintained their own mission boards. Today, the smaller, continuing mission efforts of Quakers are largely maintained through the efforts of the Yearly Meetings of Evangelical Friends International and of Friends United Meeting (Jones, 1946).

Quaker Organizations Created After World War I

In the last century, Quakers have continued to create new testimonial organizations. The pace of formation may even have increased. There certainly has been an increase in the kinds of organizations created. And Quaker organizations have intentionally reached more broadly to serve and include as full participants those who are not Quakers.

Schools and Colleges

The highpoint of Quaker schools came in the 19th century, before public schools were common, but Quakers, especially the unprogrammed Friends of Friends General Conference, continue to establish new schools. Some schools have been created in localities where none had existed before and where there had come to be Friends meetings. State College Friends School in central Pennsylvania (1943), Friends School of Atlanta (1990) and Friends School of Portland (Maine, 2006) are three examples. After World War II the desire to create integrated schools especially in places where there were strenuous efforts to preserve segregation provided a fresh impulse to the founding of Quaker schools. Thus, Carolina Friends School, was founded in 1962 by members of the Durham Friends Meeting and Chapel Hill Meeting as one of the first racially integrated schools in the South and the first in the state. More recently, Quakers have acted on concerns to provide quality pre-K education and to provide quality education for those with disabilities. Thus, Delaware Valley Friends School open in 1987 to provide secondary education for learning different students.

Today Friends Council on Education has about 80 Quaker schools in membership spread across the U.S. At least six have been founded since 2000. Friends Association for Higher Education today numbers fourteen accredited institutions of higher education among its members.

Camps

Quakers have created about two dozen camps for children and teens. Twin Rocks Friends Camp dates its founding to a 1918 gathering of Oregon Quakers at Rockaway Beach on the Pacific coast. Within a few years, they had acquired title to land at the site, and by the 1940s were maintaining summer camps for boys and girls. Quaker Haven Camp, in Syracuse, Indiana, was created in 1925 by Indiana and Western Yearly Meetings. Baltimore Yearly Meeting, operates Catoctin, Opequon and Shiloh Camps. Friends Camp was created by New England Yearly Meeting in 1953 in China, Maine, with a no longer used Meetinghouse as its first building. Like Friends schools, colleges and retirement homes, Friends camps have come to serve both Quakers and those who are not Quakers. Some Quaker camps began directly under Yearly Meeting sponsorship. Others like Camp Dark Waters in New Jersey were started as proprietary organizations that worked out an affiliation with a Yearly Meeting. (Camp Dark Waters was founded in 1927 and was privately owned until it became an independent not-for-profit in 2001.)

Retreat Centers

Over the past century, Quakers have created a number of retreat centers offering spiritual solace, workshops and programs. Pendle Hill was created outside Philadelphia in 1930. It replaced the Woolman School, which operated from 1915 to 1927. The Ben Lomand Quaker Center in California was created in 1949, and the Woolman Hill Quaker Retreat Center in Massachusetts in 1954. Beacon Hill Friends House was created in 1957 in Boston to be a center for Quaker educational activities, the home of Beacon Hill Friends Meeting, and a residential intentional community inspired by Quaker principles. New York Yearly meeting created Powell House in 1960, and in Washington, D.C., William Penn House was created in 1966.

Retirement Homes

Beginning in the 19th century, Friends created homes for retired persons, particularly those who lacked family to care for them and had played a significant role in the life of the Yearly Meeting. Some were created by Yearly Meetings, others as proprietary institutions. The Hickman, in West Chester (PA) was founded by Quakers Sallie Sharpless and Lydia Hall who saw a need to provide a safe and caring homelike environment for older single women who had no families to support them. The New England Friends Home opened in 1904 to help aging, unmarried Quaker schoolteachers. It closed in 2011 (Seltz, 2011). Stapeley Hall in the Germantown section of Philadelphia was also founded in 1904. It still serves seniors, though no longer under Quaker auspices.

Beginning in the 1960s, Quakers began creating retirement communities to provide good living settings in the manner of Friends for those in the last decades of their lives. Friends Homes in Greensboro North Carolina was founded in 1958; Friends Fellowship Community in Richmond, Indiana began in 1965. Foulkeways was created by Gwynedd Friends Meeting in 1967 as Pennsylvania's first Continuing Care Retirement Community (CCRC). In 1970, Philadelphia Yearly Meeting funded a study that led to creation of Kendal at Longwood, the first of fourteen CCRCs in the Kendal System stretched over eight states. Friends Services Alliance is an umbrella organization for several dozen Quaker organizations providing services and care for the elderly.

Quakers have also created some intergenerational, cooperative living organizations such as Pennington Friends House, founded in 1897. Friends Housing Cooperative founded in 1952 and taking up an entire city block in Philadelphia provides affordable urban living for a diverse community.

Service and Advocacy Organizations

The creation of the American Friends Service Committee in 1917 can be seen to mark a significant change in the organizational impulse among Friends. It was created for a dual purpose. One purpose was to provide an organizational framework for service by Quaker men recognized as conscientious objectors. But it also had an explicitly outward looking purpose: to undertake relief efforts in war-ravaged areas. In this it was more like a missionary effort, but with AFSC there was to be little effort to proselytize.[13]

AFSC had important British antecedents. The Friends War Victims Relief Committee was established in 1870 to provide assistance to civilians affected by the Franco-Prussian War, and then revived in response to subsequent wars in 1876, in 1912, during WWI, and again during WWII when it was renamed Friends Relief Service. Friends Ambulance Service operated during WWI and WWII. The Friends Service Council was created in 1927, and now, through

---

[13] On the new approach, see Angell (2000).

changes in organizational form and name, functions as Quaker Peace and Social Witness.

AFSC was created to meet the immediate and pressing needs arising from the First World War. After the war, the AFSC Board actively considered closing down the organization, the crisis having passed. But in the mid-1920s, it decided the good purposes it served justified its indefinite continuation.

The Friends Committee on National Legislation, the Quaker advocacy and lobbying organization was created in 1943. The Quaker United Nations Office was created in 1946 as a partnership between Friends World Committee for Consultation (which sought and received recognition by the U.N.) and the American Friends Service Committee. Quaker House, a peace advocacy organization and counseling center for those in the military was created in 1969 and located near Fort Bragg in North Carolina.

More recently, environmental issues have been a concern that has led to forming new organizations. Quaker Earthcare Witness was created in 1987, and the Earth Quaker Action Team in 2009. Recognizing that AFSC had ceased providing work camp or internship opportunities for young Quakers, Quaker Voluntary Service was created in 2009.

Interest Groups and Collaboratives

Quakers have also created a number of organizations to provide settings for discussion of topics of mutual interest. The Friends Historical Association, founded in 1873, is perhaps the oldest of these. Some others: The Friends Conference on Religion and Psychology (1943), the Fellowship of Friends of African Descent (1990), the Quaker Institute for the Future (2003), and the Quaker Religious Education Collaborative (2014).

Publishers

Joining the Friends publishers created in the early 19th century, Barclay Press was founded in 1959. In 1983, an umbrella organization was created, Quakers United in Publications, a network of Quaker publishers and booksellers.

Utilities

Quakers have also created a number of organizations to support and assist other Quaker organizations in their work. For example, Friends Fiduciary Corporation grew out of Philadelphia Yearly Meeting, became separately incorporated and now invests funds on behalf of other Quaker (and non-Quaker) organizations. The Thomas H. And Mary Williams Shoemaker Fund was first created in 1936 to provide grants for Quaker projects. Friends Center Corporation was created in 1972 to hold title to and manage the Quaker Center at 1515 Cherry Street in Philadelphia.

The Dilemmas of a Broader Reach:
What Makes an Organization Quaker?

While there still are some Quaker organizations that are "of, by and for Friends," most Quaker organizations today have a broader reach and purpose. Inclusivity and diversity are watchwords. They have grown well beyond a narrow perfect circle and believe that their Quakerness insists upon this. For example, Virginia Beach Friends School describes itself thus:

> "a community that values diversity and inclusivity, as our student body represents a wide variety of religious faiths, backgrounds and cultures. In keeping with the Quaker philosophy of honoring each individual, students representing different ethnic, cultural, religious and socioeconomic backgrounds are challenged daily to respect and learn from one another" (VBFS, n.d.)

The American Friends Service Committee says its mission is to be "a Quaker organization that promotes lasting peace with justice, as a practical expression of faith in action. Drawing on continuing spiritual insights and working with people of many backgrounds, we nurture the seeds of change and respect for human life that transform social relations and systems." (American Friends Service Committee, n.d.)

Pendle Hill declares its mission to be "a Quaker center welcoming all for Spirit-led learning, retreat, and community." (Pendle Hill, n.d.)

As Quaker organizations reach for full inclusion, what makes a Quaker organization authentically Quaker?

For the purposes of the present accounting, I have been considering as Quaker those organizations that (a) present themselves to the public as Quaker and that (b) make some explicit use of Quaker practices in their programs, governance or operations. Rarely is the question so easily settled, however. Because of their intentional, broader reach many Quaker organizations today face challenges that question their Quakerness.

For some organizations, Quakerness is more a matter of heritage than of current posture and practice. But there are disputes over legitimacy even regarding organizations that affirmatively consider themselves Quaker. Given the variety of beliefs and practices within the Religious Society today, how could these differences not spill over into questions about the authenticity of a Quaker organization? While some challenges may be idiosyncratic, five questions mark out the terrain of what makes an organization Quaker.

Can Any Organization Be Quaker?

While it may be espoused by very few, there are those who consider Quaker organizations to be impossible. For the faithful, this view holds, good works stem from leadings that arise in worship. Those leadings can only carried by individuals. Others may lend support or assistance – but only that. Any effort to institutionalize the leading robs it of legitimacy and vitality. On this view, a Quaker organization is an oxymoron.[14]

Do the Organization's Practices Conform to Quaker Testimonies?

If you visit a Friends school you are likely to encounter banners out front or posters within that lift up the Quaker testimonies as they are articulated today: simplicity, peace, integrity, community, equality and stewardship. Commitment to these is a commonly accepted indication of a Quaker organization. Some will object, however, that whatever the language used it is not Quakers alone that espouse these commitments. Commitment to the testimonies alone cannot be the distinguishing feature that makes an organization Quaker.

Do Quakers Make Up a Majority of the Governing Board?

A hundred years ago, any organization calling itself Quaker would likely have limited membership on its governing board to those who were members of the Religious Society of Friends. In recent years, any number of Quaker organizations have sought to widen the criteria for appointing board members either to include as Friends those who are associated Quaker meetings but have never sought membership, or to include those who are not Friends for their capabilities or resources. Those supporting these changes argue that there will still be a substantial number of Quakers on the board in question and that decisions will still be made via a Quaker process that seeks consensus or unity.

Is Quaker Business Practice Used?

Among organizations that explicitly present themselves as Quaker, nearly all make use of some form of Quaker business process in which decisions are reached not by majority vote but rather by seeking the active consent of all involved in making a decision. There are, however, important differences among Quaker organizations in their understanding of Quaker business practice. Some

---

[14] The most forthright presentation of this view is Tucker (1971).

see the process as seeking 'consensus,' indicating a search for a solution that re-solves or avoids disagreements within the decision-making body. This is usually a more secular understanding of Quaker business practice, one involving com-promise among individuals. Others insist that the process should be one seeking 'unity'. On this latter view, decision-making should be carried out in worship seeking the will of God, not seeking to reconcile the wants of humans.

Does the Organization Ground Itself in Worship?

Finally and most profoundly is the question of whether an organization conducts its affairs in a context of worship. Nearly all organizations that present themselves as Quakers 'take a moment of silence' as they begin business meet-ings and as they end them. For some, this gathering in silence is a matter of custom and longstanding practice. For others, it is the very heart of the matter, a shared settling into real worship, to set aside one's one wants or hopes in order to see what God wills. If an organization is to be a true Quaker organization, its purposes and approach must arise in worship and continually be refreshed in worship.

To see the Religious Society of Friends in the United States clearly to-day requires seeing both the worship and the testimonial organizations. In their history and present functioning neither can be seen as primary or dominant. At their best they nurture and support each other. One person grows up attending Meeting and later is drawn to teach at a Friends school. Another person goes to a Friends camp as a child and some decades later feels drawn to join a Quaker Meeting.

There can be tensions that arise between the two. Some of the testi-monial organizations can seem large, richly resourced and insufficiently worship-ful. Some of the worship organizations can seem insular or precious. Perhaps they have much to learn from one another.

Even as we call one set of organizations the worship fabric and another the testimonial fabric, the ethos of worship in the manner of Friends is what binds them together. We have created the worship organizations to ensure reg-ular settings for worship and care for one another; we have created the testimo-nial organizations to give substance to the concerns and leadings that arise out of worship.

As the array of testimonial organizations that Quakers have created reaches ever more broadly, "answering that of God in everyone," the central challenge facing Quaker organizations is how we connect to all peoples whatever their religious inclinations and yet sustain the life-giving insight that Quakers lift up, that God will speak to us if we still ourselves and listen (Fox, 1656, p. 263).[15]

Discussion Questions

1. Why have Quakers created so many organizations? Once created, do Quakers give these organizations the respect and support they deserve?

2. What makes an organization Quaker? Does it have to do with its programs? Its governance? Its policies and practices? Does it matter that an organization is Quaker? Why?

3. Over the years, have Quakers changed in terms of why and how they create organizations? Is this a good thing or not?

4. In what ways should we expect Quaker organizations to resemble Quaker meetings and churches? In what ways should we expect them to be different? Why?

References

Abington Friends School. (n.d.). History. Retrieved from https://www.abingtonfriends.net/about-us/history/, on May 8, 2019.

American Friends Service Committee (n.d.) Mission, vision, and values. https://www.afsc.org/mission-vision-and-values, on March 30, 2020.

Angell, S. (2000) Rufus Jones and the laymen's foreign missions inquiry: How a Quaker helped to shape modern ecumenical christianity," *Quaker Theology*, issue 3 (Fall).

Bennett, D. (2001) Race matters at Earlham," Convocation address, September 2001. https://dougbennettblog.files.wordpress.com/2011/09/race-matters-at-earlham.pdf.

Birkel, M. (2004). *Silence and witness: The Quaker tradition.* Orbis Books.

Brinton, H. (1943). *Guide to Quaker Practice.* Pendle Hill.

Bronner, E. (1967, July). Distributing the printed word: The Tract Association of Friends, 1816-1966. *The Pennsylvania Magazine of History and Biography (91)*3.

Cherry, C. (1989) *Quiet haven: Quakers, moral treatment, and asylum reform.* Farleigh Dickinson Press.

Conyers, C. (1990) *A Living legend: The history of Cheyney University, 1837-1951.* Cheyney University Press.

---

[15] For more on the larger project of which this article is a part, see https://riverview-friend.wordpress.com/quaker-organizations/.

Fox, G. (1656). *The Journal of George Fox*, ed. By John L. Nickalls. London: Religious Society of Friends.

Germantown Friends School (n.d.), Historical highlights, https://www.germantownfriends.org/about-us/historical-highlights, on May 8, 2019.

Hamm, T. (1997). *Earlham College: A History, 1847-1997*. Indiana University Press.

Hamm, T. (2003) *The Quakers in America*. Columbia University Press, 2003.

Hamm, T., Beckman, A., Florio, M., Giles, K., & Hopper, M. (2004). 'A great and good people:' Indiana Quakers and the struggle against slavery. *Indiana Magazine of History (100)*.

James, S., (1963). *A people among peoples: Quaker benevolence in 18th century America* Harvard University Press.

Jones, C. (1946). *American Friends in world missions*. Brethren Publishing House.

Kenworthy, L., (1987). The rise of Quaker education and early school. In Kenworthy, Leonard (Ed.) *Quaker Education: A Sourcebook*. Quaker Publications.

Lloyd, Arnold (1950). *Quaker Social History, 1669-1738* London: Longmans, Green

McDaniel, D., & Julye, V. (2009). *Fit for freedom, not for Friendship: Quakers, African Americans, and the myth of racial justice*. Quaker Press.

McDaniel, E., (1939). *The contribution of the Society of Friends to education in Indiana*. Indiana Historical Society.

Moore, J.M. (1974). The Centennial of the Friends Historical Association. *Quaker History 63*(1), 34-38.

Myers, M. (2012). What does it mean to be a Quaker Institution? [Presentation] Philadelphia Yearly Meeting Friends in Business, Philadelphia. Unpublished manuscript.

Oliver, J., Charles, C., and Charles, C. eds. (2007) *Founded by Friends: The Quaker heritage of 15 American colleges and universities*. Scarecrow Press.

Palmer, P. (2019). The Quaker Indian boarding schools: Facing our history and ourselves. Presentation at Pendle Hill, November 25, 2019. https://pendlehill.org/wp-content/uploads/2016/11/Quaker-Indian-Boarding-Schools.revised.pdf.

Pendle Hill (n.d.) Our vision, our mission, our values. https://pendlehill.org/explore/vision-mission-values/, on March 30, 2020.

Price, D. (1988). For 175 years: Treating mentally ill with dignity," *New York Times* April 17, 1988, p. 48.

Quakers in the World (n.d.) http://www.quakersintheworld.org/quakers-in-action/50/Influence-on-Prison-Design, on February 22, 2020.

Seltz, J. (2011, September, 8). A farewell to Friends. Boston Globe. http://archive.boston.com/news/local/articles/2011/09/08/new_england_friends_home_in_hingham_closes_its_doors

Sidwell Friends School History. (n.d.). Retrieved from https://www.sidwell.edu/about/history, on February 7, 2020.

Southland College (n.d). *Encyclopedia of Arkansas*, https://encyclopediaofarkansas.net/entries/southland-college-361/, on November 25, 2019.

The Tract Association. (2020, February 7). What is the Tract Association? https://tractassociation.org/about/, on February 7, 2020.

Trueblood, Elton (1966). *The People Called Quakers.* Harper & Row.

Tucker, R. W. (1971). Structural incongruities in Quaker service,. *Quaker Religious Thought, 27*(3).

Virginia Beach Friends School (2020, March). Small by design. https://www.vbfschool.org/about/about-vbfs/, on February 21, 2020.

Vipont, E. (1954). *The story of Quakerism, 1652-1952.* Bannisdale Press.

3| A Pedagogy of Discernment: A Journey through Social Work Values and Quaker Testimonies

By Daniel Rhodes

I. The Context

If a Quaker who has no prior knowledge of social work practice were to sit down and review social work ethics, they would see ideas and values very similar to Quaker belief and practice. The same could be said of a social worker reviewing Quaker testimonies such as peace, integrity, equality, and simplicity (AFSC, 2011). Quakers take these testimonies very seriously, and they become the foundation of their spiritual practice and growth. Quaker testimonies are not simply Bible passages to memorize; these testimonies are a way of life and being in the world. As the American Friends Service Committee (AFSC) notes,

> Quakers believe in living life in the spirit of love and truth and peace, reaching for the best in oneself and answering "that of God" in everyone. Quaker testimonies are expressions of the commitment to put those beliefs into practice (2011, p. 4).

For Quakers, these testimonies, "bear witness to the truth" (AFSC, 2011, p. 4) and are experiences that one contemplates and discerns deeply. Brazilian educator Paulo Freire understood the power of truth, or the "true word," noting that, "Thus, to speak a true word is to transform the world" (1970, p. 87). Quakers such as peace and civil rights activist Bayard Rustin understood the power of speaking truthfully when he and others authored the essay *Speak Truth to Power* for the American Friends Service Committee (Rustin, et. al., 1955).

Speaking one's truth requires commitment to contemplating and reflecting on oneself and the values that are the guiding principles in how a person lives. Queries are the mechanism Quakers use to discern the truth in their testimonies: "Quakers use queries for personal reflection, self-examination, or spirited discussion" (AFSC, 2011, p. 4). Working with social work students, it is my responsibility to mentor them in their own process of discernment when it comes to social work values. Social work students use their values as guidance in working with others, engaging in issues of social justice and working to better the world around them. Students are unable to do any of this unless they engage in a deeply reflective process of their own personal values in relation to the social work values they are to embody. In other words, social work students need to engage in a personal journey of finding their own truth and their own voice. The only way I know how to support students through this process is by example, by sharing our stories and encouraging all the students I work with to have a voice. As Freire notes, "Human existence cannot be silent, nor can it be nourished by false words, but only by true words, with which men and women transform the world" (1970, p. 88). I begin this journey with my own words and my truth.

The Beginning of the Journey

I came to social work later in life, after serving in the military and training in law enforcement. It was not a seamless transition; it evolved more out of an existential necessity. I underwent significant training up to that point, completing an associate's degree in criminal justice, acquiring skills in both the military and police training, but ultimately I discovered I was on a path that was not my own. Transitioning away from that way of life required deep contemplation and reflection on my part and shedding aspects of myself that I had worked hard to develop. Through this process of deep reflection, I also reintroduced myself to elements of who I was before I began that journey and to parts of myself that I had managed to repress.

I entered the military and studied law enforcement not because it was my passion or calling; I did it because I felt it was expected of me at that time to demonstrate I was a man. Serving for something greater than oneself at that particular time in my country's history meant military service for men. This was not my natural state, and I had to stifle much of who I really was, a person who had a strong desire for peace and social justice. I was unaware at the time, but I was discerning my path, engaging in an ontological exercise. This is not an easy exercise to undergo and can be emotionally draining, but as religious scholar John Caputo notes, "The skies do not open up and drop The Truth into our laps" (2001, p. 21).

Unmoored, I continued my education with the intent of obtaining a bachelor's degree. Unsure of an academic major, I enrolled at a local university and just started taking classes. One day, while waiting for a class to begin, I was wandering the halls looking at bulletin boards. I stumbled upon the social work department's bulletin board where various flyers were posted for graduate programs, jobs, and subsequently a list of social work values and ethics. I slowly read through them, and values jumped out at me that I had never seen before in a profession, "Community Service…Integrity…Promoting the General Welfare…" (NASW, 1993). I was amazed to see a profession that placed so much emphasis on ethical conduct and values focused on issues of social justice.

These ethical guidelines enticed me. I knew I was searching for more than just a career; I was looking for a vocation, one that placed emphasis on community, human rights and social justice. The next semester I enrolled in the introduction to social work class and declared social work as my major. This class, especially its values and ethics, had a deep impact on me, and these ethics have been my guideposts while working in the social work field. During this class I also discovered that, "Social workers have been an integral part of many movements, including civil rights, women's rights, antiwar, antiapartheid, and LGBT" (Shepard, 2015, p. 38).

This was a profound revelation for me, coming from an environment of the military (enlisting in an era when LGBTQ+ individuals were not allowed to serve) and law enforcement, with its ideology of retributive justice as opposed to social justice -- "law and order" rather than "praxis" (Freire, 2000, p. 56). It was through this class that I discovered the impact social work could have in society.

During this time, I was also deprogramming myself from the years of military and criminal justice training. I was transforming from my old self to my new self, liberating parts of myself that I had managed to tuck away and silence. Paulo Freire would call this process "conscientização" (translated as conscientization or critical consciousness), "the deepening of the attitude of awareness characteristic of all emergence" (1970, p. 109). Paulo Freire would also become a big influence in my personal and professional life. Freire's works often use terms such as "liberation" and "transformation" to describe ideas of education. "Liberation is thus a childbirth and a painful one. The man or woman who emerges is a new person…." (1970, pp. 48 – 49). This process is essential if we are to grow and develop as human beings. We cannot be stagnant creatures, blindly following the same path. "Knowledge emerges only through invention and re-invention, through the restless, impatient, continuing, hopeful inquiry human beings pursue in the world, with the world, and with each other" (Freire, 1970, p. 72).

I started seeking out spiritual traditions that were more aligned with my desire to engage in human rights and social justice. My studies brought me to

Buddhist teachings, especially the concepts of *Ahiṃsā* (non-injury or non-violence), *Karuṇā* (compassion), *Mettā* (loving kindness), and *Dāna* (giving and generosity) (Harvey, 2000). These were Buddhist ethical practices that connected very closely with social work values and helped me establish a personal ethical practice that extended beyond my profession as a social worker. The reflective practice of meditation also helped ground me during this time of transition.

Though Buddhism became my primary practice, I did pursue others in my spiritual quest, especially Christian traditions. Living in an area with historical roots in Quakerism, and geographically part of the Underground Railroad, I desired a deeper understanding of Quaker tradition. I was immediately drawn to the Quaker practice of silent worship, mirroring meditation practices I had already developed, and I was inspired by Quaker testimonies. The Quaker Peace Testimony was especially salient to me and very much aligned with my social work values and Buddhist beliefs. As the American Friends Service Committee notes, "For us, peace is not just ending war or violence, but nurturing the capacity of individuals, communities, and societies to sustain harmonious relationships based on mutual respect and caring for the welfare of all" (2011, p. 5).

There are many similarities among social work, Buddhist, and Quaker values. The similarities between Quaker and social work values are easy to discern when one looks at the background of the founder of social work, Jane Addams. Addams was heavily influenced by her Quaker father. "As a child and youth, Jane Addams drew strength from and admired her father's unshakable moral surety and his emphasis on 'mental integrity,' as he called it" (Knight, 2010, p. 10). These values have been carried down from Addams through the social work practice of today. Addams' father "may have come to his interest in perfectionism through his Quaker background....His Quakerism consisted of the lesson he taught Jane to be 'honest with yourself inside' – in other words...to trust one's inner light, rather than what others thought" (Knight, 2010, p. 10). Reisch and Andrews also point out the Quaker influence in social work, especially the more radical form of social work that I identify with, "Like the radical/reform wing of the social work profession itself, the antiwar views of radical social workers emerged from two different sources: Quaker religious values and socialist ideals" (2002, p. 41). At this point in my life, studying, contemplating, and integrating ethical ideas from these three sources were helping me develop what Paulo Freire called a "Universal human ethic" (1998, p. 23).

The Current Journey

I have been a social worker for close to 30 years now, obtaining a master's degree in social work and a clinical license (LCSW). During my tenure as a social worker, I have worked in a variety of community settings, worked with individuals with HIV/AIDS, engaged in community mental health work, worked with immigrant and refugee populations, offered therapeutic foster care, and over time shifted my practice more to community building, conflict resolution, restorative justice practices and peace work.

After obtaining my PhD, I taught at Quaker-affiliated Guilford College for four years before returning to the university where I acquired my bachelor's degree, the University of North Carolina - Greensboro. I am presently the director of the undergraduate program where I was first introduced to social work as a vocation. Social work education has become my passion, and I am dedicated to helping guide social work students into fully understanding and personally experiencing social work values. I have relied on the public intellectual bell hooks as one of my mentors in social work education. She notes,

> That learning process comes easiest to those of us who teach who also believe that there is an aspect of our vocation that is sacred; who believe that our work is not merely to share information but to share in the intellectual and spiritual growth of our students. (1994, p. 13).

I have realized during my time as a professor that traditional educational methods are ineffective when one is trying to teach students about social work values and practice. Our traditional educational model, what Freire calls the "banking" model of education, can be oppressive and will often silence students (1970, p. 72). It is through this banking model of education that teachers view students as passive recipients of information. The role of the teacher is seen as depositing knowledge and the student obediently receiving it. Freire indicates that through this banking model, "Education is suffering from narration sickness" (1970, p. 71).

This disempowering model of education alienates students from the subject matter they are learning, and the whole educational process becomes lifeless (Freire, 1970, p. 71). The main objective of the banking model of education is to contort students into "adaptable, manageable beings" (Freire, 1970, p. 73). Viewing social work students as individuals to be managed is antithetical to social work values, considering we are preparing them to go into communities and engage in dialogue with individuals and groups. As a social work educator, I do not believe we do this intentionally; we, too, were brought up in this banking model of education, so we naturally emulate it in our own teaching style because it is our "model of humanity" (Freire, 1970, p. 45). But this banking model is antidialogical, and we cannot teach students to engage in dialogue with those in the community if we are not engaging them in dialogue in the classroom. As Freire points out,

> Internalizing paternal authority through the rigid relationship structure emphasized by the school, these young people tend when they become professionals (because of the very fear of freedom instilled by these relationships) to repeat the rigid patterns in which they were miseducated. This phenomenon, in addition to their class position, perhaps explains why so many professionals adhere to antidialogical action (1970, p. 155).

For Freire "The correct method lies in dialogue" (p. 67), and "dialogue is thus an existential necessity" (1970, p. 88). Along with social work and Buddhist and Quaker values, the writings of Paulo Freire have become an indispensable part of my growth as an educator. "Freire maintained that educators should always align their values with their practices" (Leopando, 2017, p. 205). It was through this process that I began to experiment with teaching styles in the classroom. For me, following Freire's ideas, social work education must be a, "dialogical educational program concerned with social and political responsibility" (1974, p. 15). The classroom must be utilized as a living laboratory where we all engage in dialogue, not only with each other but with the very social work values we are to embody. As Freirean scholar Elias points out, "The 'ontological vocation' of persons, that is the very being or essential function of humans, is to be an active participant in the world (a subject), and not merely a passive object..." (1994, p. 55). Social work students cannot thrive in a banking model classroom; the classroom must be active and alive.

The Journey in the Classroom

At the beginning of each semester, we start the initial class session with a process I refer to as a "peacemaking circle" (Pranis, Stuart, & Wedge, 2003, p. 21). The structure of the peacemaking circle is arranged so students are positioned in a circle facing each other as opposed to the traditional banking model classroom of rows and columns, with students facing the teacher. The peacemaking circle is a form of restorative justice and serves several purposes for social work students. "Peacemaking circles are based on the process of dialogue, relationship building, and the communication of moral values in order to promote accountability, healing, and compassion through community participation in resolving conflicts" (Umbreit & Armour, 201, p. 86). Since the peacemaking circle is a restorative justice practice, it supports students in understanding that social work values are more than just theoretical. Additionally, students are now physically facing each other and have to engage in dialogue, which is foreign to those who are used to sitting in rows and columns. Through this dialogical process the social work values, especially relationship building, become a tangible, lived experience.

The banking model of education instills in students passive ways of learning that Freire calls the "security of conformity," with the teacher serving as the authoritarian figure (1970, p. 48). Utilizing the peacemaking circle, I am attempting to diffuse this hierarchical structure where I am the authoritarian figure by positioning myself in the circle with students and engaging in the same dialogical process. I cannot teach students to build relationships unless I am willing to take risks with them. "How can I motivate students unless they act with me? Inventing a course in-progress with students is both exciting and anxiety-producing" (Shore & Freire, 1987, p. 7). I am encouraging students to view my role as the educator to be "less about power-over and more about power-with" (Pranis, Stuart, & Wedge, 2003, p. 14). The unfamiliar setting of the peacemaking circle creates discomfort and ambiguity for students who are used to the banking model of education. It is in this discomfort that some of the most powerful learning experiences and personal growth can happen.

In addition to teaching students about building relationships, I am encouraging students to develop community in the classroom. If I am teaching about community and helping students learn how to work in communities, I need to cultivate community in the classroom. From a restorative justice perspective, a peacemaking circle is more than how a classroom is organized, "A circle is a way of doing things differently than we have become accustomed to. The circle is a return to our original form of community as well as a leap forward to create a new form of community" (Baldwin, 1994, p. 26).

One of the ways we begin establishing community is by creating community guidelines that we agree upon. Developing agreed upon guidelines encourages students to take responsibility for the learning environment and reinforces for students that I will also need to follow the guidelines and be a responsible member of the community. The guidelines I bring to the class to prompt students are taken from Zimmerman and Coyle's text, *The Way of Council* (2009):

1. Speaking from the heart,
2. Listening from the heart,
3. Being "lean of expression"
4. Spontaneity.

These are the initial guidelines we start with. They are written on cards placed in the middle of the circle so that we all can see and reflect on them. It is helpful if students are able to contemplate these guidelines, so to facilitate this process I have students engage in a simple mindfulness exercise in which we sit quietly, focusing on our breath. This mindful moment will only last a few minutes but is very powerful in helping students settle and be present in the moment, reflecting on the guidelines before we discuss them.

This moment of mindfulness is an opening ritual that I do at the beginning of every class I teach,

> It establishes the tone for the circle and moves participants themselves and others in different ways. It centers the person psychically and shifts his or her perspective inward from head to heart and from a focus on outer concerns to unseen forces that provide a sense of the universal connectedness of all that is. It fosters a sense of community and connection with others (Umbreit & Armour, 2011, p. 189).

This moment of mindfulness is very similar to Quaker silent reflection,

> This silent gathering is based on the belief that if one opens one's heart and listens, one can hear what is right, and can live out these inner teachings. When a group settles into silence, it feels like more than a simple quieting down; the sense of collective thought deepens (AFSC, 2011, p. 18)

It's important to note that the Quaker tradition of silent reflection and opening one's heart and listening is very much in line with the first two guidelines that I am trying to get students to embody, "speaking from the heart" and "listening from the heart." Most everything we do in educational settings is "head" centered. We are to analyze critically everything logically and objectively. Although these are important skills in education, and we need them to approach issues we deal with in life rationally, we cannot develop relationships and build community unless we are able to listen and speak from the heart. "For Freire, pedagogy has as much to do with the teachable heart as the teachable mind...." (McLaren, 2000, p.161). And for the Vietnamese Buddhist Monk, Thích Nhất Hạnh, "To repress our feelings is to repress ourselves" (p. 148). Beginning classes and teaching these mindfulness skills, or moments of silence, helps students develop the capacity to listen and speak from the heart. "Mindfulness in its totality has to do with the quality of awareness that a person brings to activities" (Linehan, 1993, p. 146).

Once we have settled in with our moment of mindfulness and have silently contemplated the guidelines, I have a talking piece I use in class that is passed around for each individual student. When students receive the talking piece, they are able to reflect on their response to the guidelines, share if there are other guidelines they feel we need to add, and agree if they are able to follow the guidelines as part of our class structure. Utilizing a talking piece allows students to have a voice and helps bring consensus about what they want out of the classroom setting -- not just what I am to bring as the authority figure.

This process helps create equity in the class, "Consequently, all participants, regardless of role or status, age, or experience, are of equal importance, with equal voice" (Umbreit & Armour, 2011, p. 179). This consensus on guidelines is a process that has been influenced by my Quaker practice of decision making: "To be effective, Quaker process requires that everyone come ready to participate fully by sharing their experiences and knowledge, by listening respectfully to the experiences and knowledge brought by others, and by remaining open to new insights and ideas." (AFSC, 2011, p. 19). These are the skills social workers will need to be effective in working with communities.

> Social workers understand that relationships between and among people are an important vehicle for change. Social workers engage people as partners in the helping process. Social workers seek to strengthen relationships among people in a purposeful effort to promote, restore, maintain, and enhance the well-being of individuals, families, social groups, organizations, and communities (NASW Code of Ethics, 2017).

My connection to Quakerism helps inform both my personal social work practice in developing relationships and teaching students how to foster relationships and engage in community work. One of the Quaker testimonies is "Community: Living in Fellowship,"

> At AFSC we nurture relationships and partner with communities, believing that, in gathering together, people increase their strength, vision, wisdom, and creativity. We accompany and support communities in their efforts to seek justice and improve their own lives and circumstances. Where people are divided, we strive to build bridges, encourage trust, and create spaces for dialogue and cooperation (AFSC, 2011, p. 11).

We can begin to see the similarities of social work values and Quaker values. Although I am not teaching Quaker values to social work students, these values have greatly influenced me and my work, which in turn impacts how I construct my classroom setting and connect with students. Developing relationships and building community are not subjects I can lecture about in class; these have to be lived experiences that students are able to reflect on in the moment.

The Journey of Reflection and Discernment

After agreeing to the guidelines, I send the talking piece around again and invite students to introduce themselves and share what brings them to social work. I feel the questions I pose are very similar to queries that Quakers use in discernment. I use this particular query for a very specific reason. Social work students are often asked why they want to be a social worker. This question engenders the response, "because I want to help people." I hear this from social work students all the time, even when I am pressing them to reflect on what kind of social work they are interested in doing. Most will fall back on the response of wanting to "help" people.

There is nothing inherently wrong with this answer, and I think it speaks to the humanitarian aspect of social work and the need many of us have of wanting to help others and work towards emolliating suffering. But there are troublesome issues that come from this "helping others" humanitarian mentality to social work, and I want to challenge students in understanding the complexities involved.

Freire cautions how humanitarian work can demarcate us from those we work with. When we approach communities, especially those that have been oppressed historically, identifying ourselves as the "helper," we are often approaching others from a paternalistic perspective that can reinforce systems of oppression (Freire, 1970, p. 54). For Freire, this paternalistic humanitarianism is hierarchical, with the "helper" being above and having power, and those being helped viewed as powerless and having little say in any course of action. In essence, paternalistic humanitarianism reinforces the historical cycle of being silenced and oppressed. Freire wants us to learn how to engage others in more "authentic" and "humanistic" ways that are liberating rather than oppressive (1970, p. 54).

Restructuring the query from why students want to be social workers, to what brought them to social work, I am encouraging students to think critically and delve more deeply into what social work means to them personally. It is also an existential endeavor, motivating students to engage in "our conversation by saying something to each other about our very existence in the world" (Horton & Freire, 1990, p. 5). This query also places students in a position to reflect on themselves and the work they will be doing, inspiring students to become what Donald Schön calls a "reflective practitioner." The query is also designed to create discomfort or a cognitive dissonance in students. They are used to responding with a simple answer that does not require much thought. Now they have to reflect on their own personal experiences and what brings them to this point in their life. I also use this as an opportunity to share about my own journey, disclosing my background and history, and the challenges I faced in becoming a social worker. This demonstrates to students that I am willing also to be vulnerable instead of just expecting them to do this on their own.

This ability to reflect deeply is an essential part of social work practice. Developing the skills of reflection is what Schön calls an "epistemology of practice" utilizing "skillful action" (1983, p. 51). It is an important concept. Engaging students in a more dialogical manner is fundamental in their development as effective social workers. As students transition to social workers entering the field and beginning to face adverse situations, they must have the skills and ability to engage in "reflecting-in-action" (Schön, 1983, p. 54). Unlike the banking model of education that disempowers students and prevents them from engaging complex situations critically, Schön notes that "reflection-in-action hinges on the experience of surprise" (1983, p. 56). Much like the importance of relationships, the ability to reflect in action is not something that can be lectured about. Instead, "reflective practice is an iterative activity which must be experienced rather than abstractly taught" (Knott & Scragg, 2016, p. 81).

The traditional banking model of education eschews emotions and attempts to legitimize itself by being defined as a form of "technical rationality…linked to principles of control and certainty. Its knowledge-constitutive interest lies in 'controlling the objectified environmental world'" (Giroux, 2001, p. 176). For those of us who teach students to become reflective practitioners, the need to understand that one cannot control the world is vital, since controlling the world would mean attempting to control those in the community one works with; there is no empathy in this. Having students reflect on what brought them to the point of deciding to become a social worker encourages them to reach inside themselves and tap into the emotional core that drives them to work with others.

Evoking an emotional response in students is part of the learning process, and "emotion is central to the reflective process" (Knott & Scragg, 2016, p. 14). This reflective process also invokes in students a sense of empathy, which moves them from the paternalistic humanitarian approach that Freire critiques to a more authentic humanist approach with a foundation on dialogue. Just helping others does not lead to much needed change, "reflection – true reflection – leads to action" (Freire, 1970, p. 66).

The Journey Towards Peace and Social Justice

> *My work with the poor and incarcerated has persuaded me that the opposite of poverty is not wealth; the opposite of poverty is justice (p. 18) Bryan Stevenson*

As indicated earlier, utilizing a peacemaking circle in class is drawing from restorative justice practices. Restorative justice is diametrically opposed to our system of retributive justice that focuses on crimes and punishment, leading to incarceration and ignoring community needs. Restorative justice focuses on harms and healing. Along with consensus for guidelines, and having students reflect on their own personal experiences, peacemaking circles focus on queries such as,

- How can we move towards healing?
- What can be done to repair the immediate harm and to prevent further harm?
- What wounds and circumstances – past and present – prevent us from having healthy relationships, both with ourselves and with others?
- What steps can we take to understand these wounds and to aid healing? (Pranis, Stuart, & Wedge, 2003, p. 11).

In other words, the peacemaking circle is a tangible way for students to understand and start developing skills for social justice work. I have found the circle process to be one of the most effective tools in helping to orient social work students to the values of social justice. The NASW guidelines (2017) emphasize that social justice is one of our key social work values,

Social workers pursue social change, particularly with and on behalf of vulnerable and oppressed individuals and groups of people. Social workers' social change efforts are focused primarily on issues of poverty, unemployment, discrimination, and other forms of social injustice. These activities seek to promote sensitivity to and knowledge about oppression and cultural and ethnic diversity. Social workers strive to ensure access to needed information, services, and resources; equality of opportunity; and meaningful participation in decision making for all people (NASW Code of Ethics).

Restorative justice is a new concept to many of our social work students. I work with them in class to help start the process of defining themselves as restorative justice practitioners. As Umbreit & Armour (2011) note, "As a social reform movement, restorative justice is social justice in action" (p. 43). Social justice is also an essential Quaker value,

We reject all forms of discrimination, whether based on race, ethnicity, nationality, religion, immigration status, class, gender, age, ability, or sexual orientation. We work to change the beliefs, practices and institutions that perpetuate prejudice, and we support affected communities in seeking their own liberation and equality (AFSC, 2011, p. 7).

Identifying oneself as a person who is concerned with issues of social justice is one thing; to actually engage in the process of confronting and challenging issues of social injustice is something entirely different. Social justice work cannot be done "to" communities; it must be done "with" communities. This is where the reflective practices I have introduced to students become essential to their social justice work. "Reflective action is crucial to challenging social injustice" (Reynolds, 2013, p. 135). Social justice work is not just "activism." Many of our social justice-oriented students like to identify themselves as activists. Freire cautions one about engaging in just simple activism, however. Working with oppressed communities is challenging, and social justice work needs a combination of theory and action, or what Freire calls "praxis" (1970, p. 65). "This discovery cannot be purely intellectual but must involve action; nor can it be limited to mere activism but must include serious reflection. Only then will it be praxis" (Freire, 1970, p. 65). For Freire praxis is "reflection and action upon the world in order to transform it" (1970, p. 51).

Freire is concerned that activism without reflection or theoretical understanding of the problem is just action, and "activism lacks a critical reflection on action" (1985, p. 11). Social justice work is more nuanced than just activism; it requires a deeper understanding of oneself and of the social injustices one is confronting (reflective practice). "Those who authentically commit themselves to the people must re-examine themselves constantly" (Freire, 1970, p. 60). It is an essential part of our social work values. "The code of conduct for social service providers calls for us to be aware of local laws and be ready to challenge those that support injustice" (Shepard, 2015, p. 77). It also requires aligning with those who are suffering from social injustice. "Political action on the side of the oppressed must be pedagogical action in the authentic sense of the word, and therefore, action *with* the oppressed" (Freire, 1970, p. 66). This is where Freire distinguishes between humanitarian work (doing to) from humanistic work (working with) (1970, p. 54.).

What becomes challenging for students is that their social justice work may conflict with the values of the places where they work. Not all social services agencies have as part of their agenda or in their mission statement confronting social injustices (or is it necessarily in the interest of the agency). In some cases, the agencies they work with may actually be creating the social injustices in the communities where social workers are working.

This discovery becomes a difficult reality for many of our social work students who begin doing community-based work their final year in the program. This is where our students come to realize that the "security of conformity" is not just something they have imposed on themselves, but that this is an issue of "structural" violence, a term coined by peace theorist Johan Galtung. For Galtung, structural violence creates "agonies caused by neglect, inaction, gross inequality and unjust structures of society, including from lack of freedom and democracy that enables people to help shape their lives" (Galtung & Fischer, 2013, p. 11).

Agencies also benefit from their workers being "adaptable, manageable beings" (Freire, 1970, p. 73). Through the process of reflection, social workers begin to realize that engaging in social justice work "may include defying the authorities in the agencies in which they work" (Shepard, 2015, p. 130). Having to process all of this in class, under safe conditions, is very theoretical for students, and their apprehension of the prospect of having to challenge the agency they may be working in while confronting social injustice in the community is palpable. Once again, this is where I am able to utilize my Quaker values in noting that "Quakers live with paradox: They are law-abiding people, but they wrote the book on civil disobedience." (Abbott, 2014, p. 14). The same can be said for social workers, and I reinforce for them that engaging in social justice means that "addressing root causes of injustice are integral to any vision of what a world at peace might look like" (Abbott, 2014, p. 27)

The Journey Continues

I teach a variety of courses on direct social work practice, with individuals, groups, and communities. During the first couple of weeks of our community-based course, I show students the documentary, *Brother Outsider: The Life of Bayard Rustin*. Most of these students have never heard of Bayard Rustin and are surprised to learn that he was one of the main architects of the Civil Rights movement and that he mentored Martin Luther King, Jr. on the philosophy and mechanics of non-violence. After viewing the documentary, we discuss why Rustin has been relegated to the sidelines of Civil Rights history: black, gay, communist, conscientious objector during WWII, Quaker. All of these come up as reasons people do not hear about Rustin as they do other Civil Rights leaders.

The scene from the documentary where King and Rustin are arguing about non-violence being an "ideology" versus a "tactic" is very powerful for students. I also enjoy watching students' reactions to Rustin thundering away that, "The only weapon we have is our bodies, and we need to tuck them in places so wheels don't turn" and his statement that, "We need in every community a group of angelic troublemakers" (Kates & Singer, 2003). This quote has become the unofficial slogan of our social work program, printed on our department t-shirts with Rustin's name and in the department cards that we send out to people. It is a quote that resonates with many of our students and permits me to begin a dialogue of how religious traditions impact the work that we do.

Greensboro has been a refugee resettlement area for over 40 years, so we have many students in our program who identify as Christian, Muslim, Jewish, Buddhist, agnostic/atheist, and other spiritual traditions. Many students acknowledge that their faith traditions or spiritual and personal "calling" is what brings them to social work. I thus work hard at honoring a student's faith tradition and encourage them to connect their own personal and religious values with social work values and ethics. This is where the dialogical process becomes vital in what I do as an educator. It is where I rely on my own personal spiritual experiences and how they have informed my social work practice. I identify as both Buddhist and Quaker, and the values of both religious traditions are important to my own personal journey and my calling as a social worker and educator.

Living in Greensboro, a community that has strong ties to Quakerism, I also discuss the history of the community in relation to slavery and how the area was part of the Underground Railroad. Many of our students from the area are unfamiliar with this rich history. In addition, our international students are excited to learn that they have relocated to a community that has a long history of fighting for human and civil rights, especially for those students who came to our community because they were escaping violence and persecution. It also allows me to open up and disclose my own connection to Quaker communities and how that has influenced my own personal social work practice. I am also able to connect students who have historically grown up steeped in more conservative ideas and, sometimes, a judgmental religious tradition, with a religious faith that is very much rooted in human rights and social justice.

I share with students that I have been trained in the Alternative to Violence Project (AVP), a training in conflict resolution and non-violence that was developed by Quakers to help educate inmates on how to engage in more effective forms of communication. I find that most of what is taught in AVP is closely aligned with what I am teaching in the class. I work closely with a group of Quakers in Jamestown, NC, who organize The North Carolina Peace Resource Center (NCPRC). NCPRC offers trainings in AVP, and I will encourage students to attend these trainings and extend academic credit if they do. The responses I have received from those who have undergone AVP training has been overwhelmingly positive. They often state that it helps them gain a deeper under-standing of what I am trying to teach in class. Many of the students have gone on to the advanced training on their own, even though they were not receiving academic credit.

Recently a representative from the Friends Committee on National Leg-islation (FCNL) organized a visit to our social work department and presented on the FCNL Spring Lobby Weekend in Washington, DC. This presenter had just graduated with his degree in social work and was working as an intern with FCNL. We had him present to a couple of our classes and scheduled times for students to meet with him to discuss his work with FCNL and about the lobbying weekend. He was effective in discussing the issues and values that FCNL advo-cates for and how closely they are in line with social work values. After his visit I worked with our social work student organization to help a group of students attend the upcoming FCNL Lobby Weekend. Students were very excited that they would have an opportunity to travel to DC and receive training on how to lobby for issues that are very important to social workers. My goal is to continue to offer this opportunity yearly for students who are interested.

I also share with students about traveling to Palestine/Israel and staying in the occupied Palestinian territories while there. I have traveled to this region three times with Friends United Meeting "Living Letters" service-learning groups led by Jane and Max Carter. We stay at the Ramallah Friends School, and I share about the history of Quakers working towards non-violent solutions be-tween Palestinians and Israelis. I confide with students how these have been life changing trips and how we meet with different human rights groups and organ-izations who are utilizing non-violence in responding to the situation. One ex-ample is Al-Haq (justice and truth), "an independent Palestinian non-govern-mental human rights organization based in Ramallah, West Bank. Established in 1979 to protect and promote human rights and the rule of law in the Occupied Palestinian Territory (OPT)" (Al-Haq). Another is the Parents Circle – Family Forum (PCFF),

> A joint Israeli-Palestinian organization of over 600 families, all of whom have lost an immediate family member to the ongoing conflict. Moreo-ver, the PCFF has concluded that the process of reconciliation between nations is a prerequisite to achieving a sustainable peace (PCFF).

Most of our students are greatly misinformed about the conflict in this area and are amazed to hear of Arab Muslims and Christians living and working for peace and justice alongside Israeli Jews. They are surprised by the complexity of the conflict. It reinforces for them that human rights and social justice are global issues and that as social workers they have to take an international view in the work they do in communities.

As Elias (1994) cogently points out, "To exist means to transcend, discern, and enter into dialogue" (p. 35). With my dialogical process in the classroom, I am attempting to get social work students to understand that becoming a social worker is more than just "helping people;" in many ways it is a calling. I cautiously do this by walking a fine line between the secular approach at a public university system and honoring students where they are in their own personal and faith traditions. Utilizing Freire helps me do this because his "world view can be described as a Christian-Marxist humanism" (Elisa, 1994, p. 47) or what Freire himself calls a "scientific revolutionary humanism" (1970, p. 133). This is where the praxis of my role as educator comes in and why I use the circle process with students in helping them to discern why they are called to be social workers, and why that calling is not a singular act, but an ongoing, evolving process that people experience daily. I think Freire sums this up best,

> What makes men and women ethical is their capacity to 'spiritualize' the world, to make it either beautiful or ugly. Their capacity to intervene, to compare, to judge, to decide, to choose, to desist makes them capable of acts of greatness, of dignity, and, at the same time, of the unthinkable in terms of indignity. It's not possible to break with an ethical code unless one has become an ethical being (1998, p. 53).

Discussion Questions

1. There are many similarities between Quaker testimonies and social work values. What are some of the similarities between the two?

2. Much like Quakers "discerning" Quaker testimonies, social workers need to discern social work values and ethics. Why is it important for social workers to discern their values in the work that they do?

3. Paulo Freire highly valued dialogical interaction in the educational setting, resisting the idea of students becoming "adaptable, manageable beings." Why is this form of Freirean dialogue so vital for social workers engaging in community-based work?

4. While engaging in the Civil Rights movement Bayard Rustin noted that "We need in every community a group of angelic troublemakers." How would a statement like this resonate with social workers in the community?

References

Abbott, M. P. (2014). *A theological perspective on Quaker lobbying*. FCNL.

Al-Haq (2010, October 16). *About Al-haq*. AL-HAQ: Defending Human Rights. http://www.alhaq.org/about-alhaq/7136.html

American Friends Service Committee (2011). *An introduction to Quaker testimonies*. AFSC Publishing.

Baldwin, C. (1994). *Calling the circle: The first and future culture*. Bantam Books.

Caputo, J. D. (2001). *Thinking in action: On religion*. Routledge Publishing.

Elias, J. L. (1994). *Paulo Freire: A pedagogue of liberation*. Krieger Publishing.

Freire, P. (1970). *Pedagogy of the oppressed*. Bloomsbury Publishing.

Freire, P. (1974). *Education for critical consciousness*. Continuum Impacts Publishing.

Freire, P. (1985). *The politics of education: Cultural power and liberation*. Bergin & Garvey Publishing.

Freire, P. (1998). *Pedagogy of freedom: Ethics, democracy, and civic courage*. Rowman & Littlefield Publishing.

Freire, P. (2000). *Cultural action for freedom*. Harvard Educational Review.

Galtung, J., & Fischer, D. (2013). *Johan Galtung: Pioneer of peace research*. Springer Publishing.

Giroux, H. (2001). *Theory and resistance in education: Towards a pedagogy for the oppressed*. Bergin & Garvey Books.

Harvey, P. (2000). *An introduction to Buddhist ethics*. Cambridge Press.

Hooks, B. (1994). *Teaching to transgress: Education as the practice of freedom*. Routledge Press.

Horton, M., & Freire, P. (1990). *We make the road by walking: Conversations on education and social change*. B. Bell, J. Gaventa, & J. Peters (Eds.). Temple University Press.

Kates, N., & Singer, B. (Producers) (2003). *Brother outsider: The life of Bayard Rustin* [Motion Picture]. USA. Corporation for Public Broadcasting.

Knight, L. W. (2010). *Spirit in action: Jane Addams*. W. W. Norton & Company Publishing.

Knott, C., & Scragg, T. (2016). *Reflective practice in social work* (4th ed.). SAGE Publishing.

Leopando, I. (2017). *A Pedagogy of faith: The theological vision of Paulo Freire*. Bloomsbury Publishing.

Linehan, M. (1993). *Cognitive Behavioral Treatment for Borderline Personality Disorder*. The Guilford Press.

McLaren, P, (2000). *Che Guevara, Paulo Freire, and the Pedagogy of Revolution*. Rowman & Littlefield Publishing.

National Association of Social Workers (1993). *NASW Code of Ethics*. https://www.socialworkers.org/LinkClick.aspx?fileticket=Q WqndhwcVt8%3d&portalid=0

National Association of Social Workers (2017). *NASW Code of Ethics*. https://www.socialworkers.org/about/ethics/code-of-ethics/code-of-ethics-english

Parent Circle – Family Forum (2019). https://www.theparentscircle.org/en/about_eng/

Pranis, K., Stuart, B., & Wedge, M. (2003). *Peacemaking circles: From crime to community*. Living Justice Press.

Reisch, M., Andrews, J. (2001). *The road not taken: A history of racial social work in the United States*. Routledge Publishing.

Reynolds, W. M. (2013). Liberation theology and Paulo Freire: On the side of the poor. In R. Lake, & T. Kress (Eds.). *Paulo Freire Intellectual Roots: Towards Historicity in Praxis*. Bloomsbury Publishing.

Rustin, B. (1955). *Speak Truth to Power: A Quaker search for alternative to violence*. American Friends Service Committee.

Shepard, B. (2015). *Community projects as social activism: From direct action to direct service*. SAGE Publishing.

Schön, D. (1983). *The reflective practitioner: How professionals think in action*. Basic Books Publishing.

Shore, I., & Freire, P. (1987). *A pedagogy for liberation: Dialogues on transforming education*. Bergin & Garvey Publishers.

Stevenson, B. (2014). *Just mercy: A story of justice and redemption*. Spiegel & Grau Publishing.

Thích Nhất Hạnh (2012). *Awakening of the heart: Essential Buddhist sutras and commentaries*. Parallax Press.

Umbreit, M., & Armour, M. P. (2011). *Restorative Justice dialogue: An essential guide for research and practice*. Springer Publishing.

Zimmerman, J. & Coyle, V. (2009). *The way of council* (2nd Ed.). Bramble Books.

4| Elizabeth Fry—Prison Reformer and a Quaker of Note

By Paul Anderson

Her picture is on the five-pound British note. She brought about prison reform in Britain, which spread to civilized nations in Europe and beyond. Her school of nursing inspired and supported the work of Florence Nightingale. She was the first woman to address Parliament and did so several times. She was visited in her prison-reform work by kings and queens of Denmark and Prussia. She was a recorded Friends minister who provided Bibles for people, established multiple organizations for social reform, challenged the death penalty and slavery, and who was sponsored by Queen Victoria. Referred to as "the Angel of the Prisons" (Richards, 1916), her name was Elizabeth Fry—a *note-worthy Friend*, indeed!

Elizabeth Fry's Upbringing, Convincement, and Calling

Born into a Quaker banking family in Norwich, England, Elizabeth Gurney (1780-1845) was raised with a respect for Christian living and the values found in Scripture. Robert Barclay was her great grandfather on her mother's side (Catherine Bell), and ancestors on her father's side (John Gurney) had been followers of George Fox. Nonetheless, young Elizabeth struggled at times to follow in the ways of devotion; in her journal she expressed concern over such "wicked inclinations" as flirting, anger, exaggeration, and giving way to luxury. As a 17-year old, however, when Quaker evangelist William Savery engaged the Gurney family on a ministry tour to England, Elizabeth was convinced of the truth and gave her life to Christ. In her own words,

To-day I have felt that *there is a God!* I have been devotional, and my mind has been led away from the follies that it is mostly wrapped up in. We had much serious conversation; in short, what he said, and what I felt, was like a refreshing shower falling upon earth that had been dried for ages. (Fry & Cresswell, 1974, p. 36)

William Savery had also prophesied that Elizabeth would make a difference for God in the world, and while that prediction did come to pass, the way forward was not exactly direct. The fourth child among eleven surviving children, Elizabeth's mother died when she was twelve. Her mother, however, read the Bible to her children mornings and evenings, and responsibility for teaching biblical stories and truths to her younger siblings fell largely to Elizabeth and her older sister, Catherine. As Earlham Hall served as a center of social events involving music, dancing, and other forms of entertainment more conducive to higher society than the plain practices of Friends, young "Betsy" found herself resisting pressures to commit herself to traditional Quaker challenges to vanity and ostentation. To be fair, she also felt that some of her social gifts and graces would be underserved if she were to commit to plainness; she enjoyed singing and loved her purple boots with scarlet laces, which she also wore to meeting. One of the family friends that visited Earlham Hall from time to time was Prince William Frederick, nephew of King George III, and the Gurneys were known to all levels of British society. To say that the Gurneys were in tension with the plainness testimonies of Friends at that time would be an understatement.

The Gurney clan thus represents one of the most ironic tensions experienced by leading Friends of the 19th century. Testifying against showy habits of wealthy societal leaders from the perimeter is one thing; maintaining Christian Testimonies against ostentation from the aristocratic inside is another. The Gurney family had managed woolen mills in East Anglia for several generations, leading to the developing of banking enterprises serving to manage investments and transactions. Because the Gurneys and other Quaker bankers were honest and trustworthy, their banks became leaders in the industry. In 1896 some twenty Quaker banks and companies were consolidated into Barclays Bank. As the Gurney family had become known for its wealth, the Gilbert and Sullivan opera, *Trial by Jury* (1875), references someone who would become "as rich as the Gurneys." As was said of Friends elsewhere, they went to Philadelphia to do good…, and, they *did well*. The reverse, however, is also true. Because of having done well, faithful Friends also enhanced their capacities to do good.

In addition to banking and textile mills, Quaker families also became leaders in business and industry—including such fields as iron making, railways, ceramics, pharmaceuticals, insurance, and chocolate. They also took the lead in social work and justice reforms—including such concerns as education, healthcare, abolition, suffrage, nonviolence, temperance, and prison reforms. Along these lines, the Darby, Reynolds, Barclay, Gurney, and Fry families exemplified these tandem ventures, perhaps even seeing effective service in business and industry as creating the opportunity for, and even the responsibility to further, social service, gospel ministry, and justice reforms in the world.

Having moved into Earlham Hall in 1786, the Gurney home became known as "one of the happiest homes in England," a social center for the region (Bayne, 1869, p. 104). They often held concerts, dancing, and other hospitality events in their home, and the Gurney children were unconvinced regarding the traditional plainness testimonies of Friends. Influenced by writers during the age of reason, young Elizabeth had also come to question the reality of God and whether the Bible was true. Her mother read the Scriptures to the children, but Elizabeth had yet to find personal meaning in the texts. And, while the family was regular in attending the Friends Meeting, the children commented on feeling bored and disinterested overall. They referenced the meeting for worship as "dis" (disgusting), and they demurred against the judgment they felt from plain Quakers, as they felt more at home among the upper echelons of society.

Elizabeth's doubts, however, were overcome by spiritual encounters precipitated by the ministry of the traveling American Friend, William Savery, whose ministry at Goat Lane Meeting made a profound impression upon young Elizabeth. When two hundred Friends gathered to receive his ministry, the front row was occupied by all seven Gurney girls, dressed in colorful garb and fashion. In Savery's reflection, "I thought it the gayest meeting of Friends I ever sat in, and was grieved to see it" (Savery, 1869, p. 278). Thus taken back at the "gaiety" of well-to-do Friends at the Norwich meeting ("gay Friends" were distinguished from "plain Friends"—the former wearing colors and fashionable clothing, the latter wearing gray or black and more simple clothing), Savery's challenges regarding ostentation, social investments, and frivolities struck home in Elizabeth's conscience. As he himself was a recent convert to the "plain" way of Friends, Savery spoke from experience about his convincement regarding the humble way of Christ.

Following the meeting, Elizabeth followed Savery and others to her uncle's home for lunch, and according to her sister, she was reduced to tears on the way home in the carriage because she was spiritually moved. Savery joined the Gurney family for breakfast the next morning and spent a good deal of the day affirming gospel values and the essence of true religion—a direct contrast to writings familiar to the Gurneys by Thomas Paine, David Hume, and the deists. This continued to have a profound spiritual impact upon Elizabeth, whose heart was touched by Savery's convicting but nonjudgmental witness to Christian concerns. As she rode with him to meeting in a carriage, the conversation led to feeling a sense of "meeting" that was confirmed by the gathering itself. In America, Savery had been a defender of Native Americans' rights; during his ministry in Europe, he addressed concerns for the poor and the disadvantaged. He reports challenging his audience at Norwich to "choose the simple, safe path of self-denial" over and against "the alluring things of this world" (Savery, 1869, p. 279).

Soon thereafter, Elizabeth's father accompanied her on a trip to London, where she enjoyed the amusements of theater, concerts, and dancing. In addition to connecting his daughter with the larger social scene, this and other trips served to season Elizabeth's sense of direction and calling. While she reports enjoying the social life of the big city, and her excitement over catching glimpses of the Prince of Wales at events, she also worried that her liberties would be judged negatively by plain Friends in London. When Elizabeth heard William Savery speak again at Westminster Friends Meeting, his witness piqued her conscience further. She thus records in her journal that her interest in theater and concerts had waned, while her leadings to become a plain Friend had grown.

Upon returning to Earlham Hall, Elizabeth traveled West with her father, visiting Friends at Bath, Coalbrookdale, and elsewhere. Her older cousin, Priscilla Hannah Gurney, had asserted winsome influence regarding plainness, and her witness solidified Elizabeth's commitment along those lines. She reports this visit as being one of the happiest experiences in her life, and apparently a number of things came together in terms of her sense of calling. As she may have been dyslexic and suffered fears of the dark, drowning, and death, she now felt released from those fears and their accompanying dreams. At Coalbrookdale, the noted public minister and interpreter of Scripture, Deborah Darby, prophesied that Elizabeth would be "a light to the blind; speech to the dumb; and feet to the lame." In staying on for several days after her father left, Elizabeth felt called to be "a minister of Christ," a vocation that set the trajectory of the rest of her life.

Marriage, Family Life, and Education

Following her visit to Coalbrookdale, Elizabeth was approached by Joseph Fry, whom she'd earlier met in London, as to the prospect of marriage. She was divided on the issue, however, fearing that it would encroach upon her sense of calling to ministry. She also worried about her "faults" and expressed that concern in general terms to her suitor, who eventually won her over nonetheless. In the meantime, Elizabeth's sense of calling to ministry developed in response to particular needs and concerns. For instance, in attending the last hours of a dying servant named Bob, Elizabeth read him a chapter from the Bible, which seemed to speak to his condition. This was followed by a concern to educate the underprivileged children in the Norwich area, later inspired by her visit to Ackworth School (August 1799) and seeing how children were educated there. She thus opened the laundry room of Earlham Hall as a First Day School (September 1798), teaching over seventy disadvantaged children to read. They also read the New Testament aloud, serving to "increase morality" among them. They were affectionately called "Besty's imps" by her siblings, and a week before her wedding, eighty-six of them showed up to say goodbye and to wish her well. Some of them shed tears over her departure to London, and Betsy reports also having shed a few tears for them after they departed.

On August 19th 1800, Elizabeth was married to Joseph Fry at the age of 20. Son of William Stores Fry, Joseph was a tea merchant and banker; he and his family were plain Friends. Following the wedding at Goat Lane Meeting, the couple moved to London, where they occupied the family home above the counting house of Mildred's Court in London's banking district. Over the next two decades, Elizabeth gave birth to eleven surviving children, seeking also to raise them with a good education and values and a knowledge of Scripture. She would read the Bible to them on a daily basis, even when they had guests in their home. She also insisted on reading the Bible aloud for the benefit of all present when they traveled to Scotland, France, and elsewhere (Larsen, 2011, pp. 174-75). In so doing, she followed the concern of Friends at the time, who sought to recover the primary place of Scripture in persons' spiritual lives, committing to the discipline of daily Bible reading for inspiration and guidance. Elizabeth was present at the establishment of the *British and Foreign Bible Society* in 1804, and when the *Norwich Auxiliary of the Bible Society* was established in 1811, Joseph John Gurney served as an organizer of the event, and the interdenominational reception was held at Earlham Hall.

Life in the Fry home was full, offering hospitality to traveling Friends, including those attending the Yearly Meeting Sessions each May in London. At times they served as many as sixty guests at table, and their extension of hospitality was seen as a ministry to those traveling from afar. In addition to raising her children, Elizabeth became inspired by the peer-tutoring approach to educating the underprivileged children of London, pioneered by Joseph Lancaster. Having experimented for several years with a monitor-based system of education, whereby a master teacher would teach lead-students who would in turn pass along their learnings to other students, Lancaster opened up a Free School in

London in 1798.[1] This school grew to serving as many as a thousand students, and it inspired Elizabeth to work toward educating poor children locally and beyond.

In 1806, Gracechurch Street Friends Meeting appointed her a *visitor to the Quaker school and workhouse at Islington*, founded by John Bellers at Clerkenwell a century earlier (later moved to Croydon). Elizabeth served the school by providing Bible readings, distributing religious tracts, and helping them develop constructive games. She also provided them with clothes and helped organize their ways of maintaining cleanliness and hygiene. After she read to the children, they were deeply moved with appreciation, for which she could only give thanks. In addition to lending her support to the school's work, her visits further bolstered her vision of how children might be educated well. Even so, she describes the labor of her volunteer work, household management, and motherhood challenging her calling to be "a useful instrument of the Church Militant," as she also felt herself also to be "a care-worn wife and mother." Nonetheless, over her lifetime, she founded and supported several schools and educational ventures, believing strongly that the best way to help the poor was to provide them the means of making an honest contribution to society, which would also bolster employability and enterprising skills.

Following the death of Joseph's father in 1809, the family moved to Plashet House estate, about eight miles away. Near East Ham in the country, Plashet House offered a more nature-friendly setting than the city center. The planting of flowers and the cultivation of gardens allowed the family to enjoy the natural surroundings, reminding Elizabeth of her earlier days at Earlham Hall. One of the first things Elizabeth did after the move was to organize a school for the education of children in the area. Directly opposite the gate of the property, a large dwelling was occupied by an elderly couple who had fallen on hard times financially. Several of the rooms were unoccupied, and the family was eking out an existence by the raising and selling of rabbits. Elizabeth raised her concern for the uneducated poor with them in the region and offered them rent for the use of their largest room as a school. In so doing, the children in the area were availed an education, and the couple was helped financially.

Elizabeth also took a personal interest in the poor Irish and Gypsy people living in the area, and she was befriended dearly by their communities. She

---

[1] First published in 1803, Lancaster's booklet, *Improvements in Education*, lays out the history and theory of his approach toward educating the masses. See the fuller version: *Improvements in Education, as it Respects the Industrious Classes of the Community: With a Brief Sketch of the Life of Joseph Lancaster by William Corston* (Cambridge: Cambridge University Press, 2014).

investigated new ways of combatting the dreaded smallpox blight by inoculating her own and other children in the area with cow pox. As a result, smallpox was virtually eliminated from the area. She established a soup kitchen at Plashet House as a means of feeding those in need, and she supported the establishment of several additional schools in the area. Indeed, she sought to elevate the state of the entire community by instituting appropriate educational and social reforms as a direct expression of her ministerial calling.

That same year, Elizabeth's father died, and at the memorial service, she felt led to lead out in prayer, expressing thanksgiving and dedication to the Lord's service. In so doing, she quoted Revelation 15:3 from memory, proclaiming, "Great and marvelous are Thy works, Great God Almighty: just and true are all Thy ways, Thou King of Saints; be pleased to receive our thanksgiving." From that time on, Elizabeth felt released to engage in public ministry, and she was recorded as a Friends minister in London Yearly Meeting in 1811. A good deal of her public ministry simply involved her reading biblical texts aloud, allowing the truth of Scripture to speak for itself, as the life-giving Word of God within.

While Quakers had wrongly been understood as devaluing the Bible because of their prioritizing the workings of the Spirit who inspired the texts, Elizabeth and her brother Joseph John Gurney demonstrated a high view of the Bible's capacity to inspire and to convey transformative truth. In that sense, the interpretation of Scripture was seen as a direct response to the inspired text in deeds and organizing work, rather than debating theological points and counterpoints. And, if Matthew 25 were to be taken seriously, which Elizabeth Fry certainly did, seeing Christ among the naked, the imprisoned, and the sick evoked a call to action, not simply contemplation. She thus viewed her social work and reform programs as direct responses to the convicting content of the biblical text, putting faith into practice.

Newgate and Prison Reform

During the War of 1812 and the Napoleonic War, many businesses and banks went bankrupt, and the Fry's bank faced a number of financial hardships. Financial pressures during the winter of that year led to the family's moving back to Mildred's Court, which brought them into contact with Stephen Grellett, whose traveling ministry brought him to London. In January of 1813, he visited Newgate Prison along with William Allen and Peter Bedford. They were terribly disturbed at the plight of the prisoners, especially the women, and Grellett directly shared with Elizabeth about the horrific conditions of the prisoners. She had visited the prison in Norwich with her father as a child, and Quakers' concerns for the imprisoned went back to the first days of the movement. Friends suffered imprisonment for standing up to their religious convictions and were well acquainted with prison ministries. In particular, Newgate was described as "Hell above ground," and it was said that its "horror, filth and cruelty would have disgraced even a slave ship." As Alice Almond Schrock (2016, p. 29) described it,

> First to assault the senses was the stench: daily human waste, menstrual blood, birthing blood, alcohol, vomit all saturated the floor straw and produced an overwhelming odor. Then came the racket: the screaming and fighting of the felons crammed into windowless wards built for 60 but containing 300 women and children.

Upon hearing about the dismal plight of the women and children in the prison, Elizabeth immediately sprang into action. Calling together several women to assist her and ordering bolts of flannel, they made clothes for the children and delivered them to the prison the next day. Following her visit, Elizabeth described being deeply troubled by the conditions: "…the filth, the closeness of the rooms, the furious manner and expressions of the women towards each other, and the abandoned wickedness…" (Jowett, 2017, p. 97). The jailer protested, concerned for her safety, but Elizabeth declared that while she was fully aware of the danger, "I do not go on my own strength. God will protect me" (Hale, 1842, p. 305). Reflecting on her first visit later, she recounts reading to the inmates Luke 7-15, beginning with Jesus being criticized for dining with sinners and concluding with the Parable of the Prodigal Son. Indeed, she won over the hearts and minds of the inmates by simply offering, "I am come to with a wish to serve you, if you will allow me" (Hale, 1842, p. 305).

The plight was especially dismal for women and children in Newgate, many of whom had been born in prison. The "turnkey" wardens exacted a cruel "garnish" bribe, whereby they charged incoming inmates to pay a fee, and if they had no money, they were expected to hand over parts of their clothing. Thus, many women were only partially clad, and children had no clothing at all. Elizabeth was disturbed by women removing clothes of a dead child so that others could have at least some clothing. Prison guards also took advantage of their access to women sexually, but Newgate was not alone in this abuse. As Elizabeth visited prisons in France and other nations several years later, in Montpelier, for instance, they found two women who had been impregnated by the guard. Male guards at times regarded women's prison wards as their personal brothel. She thus campaigned for female supervisors of female prisoners, and she also worked for the abolishment of the public flogging of women, campaigns that were eventually successful.

Over the next few months, Elizabeth visited the prison several more times, reading the Bible to groups of inmates and encouraging them to embrace the moral virtues described therein. However, over the next three and a half years, financial pressures at home, giving birth to several more children, and caring for young "Betsy" who died as a five-year-old demanded her time and attention, kept her away. With Elizabeth's return to the scene around Christmas of 1816, she reported that whereas the women had been "like wild beasts" beforehand, they now "appear harmless and kind." She prayed for the women, and they gathered around her on their knees in appreciation for her loving concern. She later picked up a child and asked what might be done to help these innocent ones; that gesture led to interest in organizing a school within the prison.

In April of 1817, Elizabeth founded the *Association for the Improvement of the Female Prisoners of Newgate*, and things really began to change. The Association consisted of eleven Quaker women and the wife of a clergyman (likely Karl Steinkopf, foreign secretary of the British and Foreign Bible Society; Larsen, 2011). They arranged support for clothing, food, Bibles, and other supplies for enhancing the well-being of the prison population. They organized a school within the prison itself, tasking more able women as monitors who would teach children and other women to read. She divided the inmates into groups of twelve (following the pattern of the twelve disciples), appointing a matron at the head of each group, encouraging local self-management and care. The Bible was read at the beginnings and endings of every day, and the moral tone of the inmates began to change. Inmates were also encouraged to take responsibility for cleaning and setting things in order, which enhanced the livability of their quarters and the wellbeing of the inmates.

In thinking strategically about how to create systems of reform and accountability within the prison itself, and this led to devising a set of rules for reform. Mary Connor was appointed and financially supported as the head teacher and overseeing superintendent, and the following rules were implemented.

1. A matron would be appointed for overseeing the women
2. Women would be engaged in knitting, needlework, and other suitable employment
3. No begging, swearing, gambling, card playing, quarreling or immoral conversation
4. A yard-keeper would keep track of women's behaviors and issues, reporting to the matron
5. Women would be divided into classes of not more than twelve

6. Monitors would be chosen among the women, being orderly, responsible, and able to read
7. Monitors oversee the behaviors of women and hold them accountable before the matron
8. Monitors breaking rules would be replaced by another who was faithful
9. Monitors should insure that woman have clean hands and faces, being also quiet in their work
10. At the 9:00 ringing of the morning bell, women should gather for the reading of Scripture, followed by instruction and work
11. At 6:00 women would gather for the evening reading, followed by monitors reporting to the matrons on the work done that day
12. The matron will keep an exact account of the work and behavior of each woman, reporting also to the Association (Fry, 1828, pp. 17-19)

The prison authorities doubted whether such a program could succeed, but its results were astounding. When these rules were proposed to the women, all the hands went up in unanimous support of the plan. No punishments were levied, but people were held accountable simply by means of oversight and reporting on conditions and performance. The success astounded the wardens and those in charge of London's prisons. The Association raised funds from the Gurneys and other sources to provide women with Bibles and reading materials, with sewing materials, and with food. As the prisoners were given meaningful tasks to do, this also led to their earning money. Within less than a year, over 20,000 items of clothing were produced by the women at Newgate, and a contract with Richard Dixon and Company came through, providing clothing for women convicts being transported to Australia. In 1821, this organization was expanded into the first *national women's society*, which expanded the concerns nationally: *the British Ladies' Society for Promoting the Reformation of Female Prisoners.*

When a visitor toured the prison around this time, he was amazed that there was no quarrelling or fighting among the prisoners, and that the quarters were clean and well maintained. What he observed was a stately woman reading the Bible to some sixteen women, who were engaged in embroidery and needlework. When he entered, they rose and greeted him respectfully, each dressed in a blue apron, bib, and cap. Another visitor reflected upon Elizabeth's empathic reading of Isaiah 53, where the suffering of the Redeemer is said to further the healing of later generations. Women were moved to tears at her reading, which was likely similar to her later recording of one of her sermons:

> Indeed, it is well for us, my friends, to enquire, "What owest thou unto thy Lord?" Ah, dear friends, is it not well for us to do this when we

reflect on what he hath done for us, even He who was wounded for our transgressions, who was bruised for our iniquities; the chastisement of our peace, we may remember, was on him, and by his stripes we are healed. It is well for us to remember what he hath been from time to time doing for us in the visitations of his love unto our souls; how often have the proofs of his love been extended towards us to gather us and keep us within his sacred enclosure, even the revelation of the will of God through Jesus Christ our Lord, our hope of glory. (Leng, 2006, pp. 144-45)

Newgate was something of a holding station. Prisoners were to suffer one of several fates: be acquitted, transferred, shipped overseas, or executed. On the latter item, public hangings were promoted and attended as public events. Elizabeth Fry, however, believed for any "man to take the prerogative of the Almighty into his own hands," in terms of *capital punishment*, was wrong. At the time, there were over 220 crimes for which a person could be executed in England, and most of them were petty. Grieved over the execution of a mother with seven children and another woman who had actually killed her baby, Elizabeth sought to intervene in the execution of Harriet Skelton, who was accused of forging a check. Because she was carrying out her husband's wishes she did not plead guilty to the minor account, but this inadvertently led to her death sentence.

Elizabeth pleaded her case to Lord Sidmouth, the Home Secretary and to the Duke of Gloucester, but to no avail. She was even granted an audience with Queen Charlotte at London's Mansion House, the home of the Lord Mayor. While the Queen was supportive of her concerns, she did not intervene. Lord Sidmouth resented the pressure placed upon him by those in high places, and Harriet was hanged shortly thereafter. Nonetheless, Elizabeth was able to meet with her the day before her passing. Along with her brother, Joseph John Gurney, Elizabeth and other Friends campaigned hard against the death penalty in England. In 1823 the *Judgment of Death Act* was passed by Parliament, granting judges leeway in death sentences other than murder and treason, thus reducing the number of capital crimes from over two hundred to two. Public executions were eliminated in 1868, and the death penalty was eventually limited further by law.

As news spread about the transformation of Newgate Prison, interest grew locally and abroad. Her *Friday Bible readings* had become so popular that a ticket system had to be devised to accommodate the interest in an orderly way. Leaders within the United Kingdom and beyond wondered what could also be done to improve the conditions of prisons elsewhere. Four decades earlier, John Howard had published a report on the sad state of England's prisons (1777), but the work of Elizabeth Fry carried his work further by actually implementing re-forms effectively and calling for legal reforms. When the Lord Mayor and the Sheriffs of London visited her in the Newgate Prison, they found her in a clean white-washed room reading the Bible to a group of women who were quiet and attentive. What chains and fetters could not accomplish, a woman dressed in plain clothing could. After consultation with the Emperor of Russia, reforms were instituted in Saint Petersburg. A new prison was being constructed, pat-terned after the prison reforms Elizabeth had advanced, including providing Bi-bles in prisoners' cells. In 1822, the Princess of Denmark came to visit Elizabeth Fry for breakfast, hoping to learn more about her prison work, and her influence was sought in Italy, France, Netherlands, Germany, and Prussia. Upon his visit to Newgate that same year, John Randolph, the American Senator and Ambas-sador to Russia declared:

> Two days ago I saw the greatest curiosity in London, and in England too, compared to which Westminster Abbey, the Tower, Somerset House, the British Museum, nay Parliament itself, sink into utter insig-nificance. I have seen Elizabeth Fry in Newgate, and I have witnessed there the miraculous effect of true Christianity upon the most depraved of human beings. (Garland, 1869, p. 185)

Elizabeth's brother in law, Thomas Fowell Buxton now a member of Parliament, had been assisting her in the prison work at Newgate and published his own book: *Inquiry into Prison Discipline*.[2] He then invited her to address the Commission on the state of British prisons the House of Commons in February 1818. She was the first woman to address Parliament, and she would do so several times further. In 1826, she reported to the Police Committee and in 1832 to the Prisons Committee of the House of Commons. And, in 1835 she testified before a Select Committee of the House of Lords, arguing that while severe punishment might deter some from crime, the changing of the human heart and real reformation happens by administering biblical truths, which transform the individual from within.

Of course, Elizabeth Fry's concerns were not rooted only in her expe-rience at Newgate; she traveled extensively throughout the United Kingdom and Europe over several decades, making no fewer than five visits to Europe between 1838 and 1843. In August of 1818, Elizabeth with one of her daughters and Jo-seph John and his wife Jane Gurney toured prisons in the north of England and in Scotland, and their report exposed the dismal state of prison conditions na-tionwide (Gurney, 1819). What they found is that the conditions of prisons in

---

[2] The full title is longer (Edinburgh: Archibald Constable and Company, 1818).

the north were even worse than those at Newgate, so reforms needed to be sweeping and just.

In 1827, Fry visited women prisoners in Ireland, and she toured Germany, France, Netherlands, Prussia, and other nations over the next decade and a half. In 1842, Frederick William IV of Prussia visited Elizabeth Fry, taking note of her work at Newgate Prison. By now she had become the most famous woman in all of Europe, and she also played a formative role in developments within the Brtitish monarchy. Having encouraged her to consider the lot of Josiah who became king as a child, Elizabeth had won the sympathies of Princes Victoria before she became Queen in 1837. Queen Victoria later supported Elizabeth's halfway-house work with a modest financial contribution, but even more significantly, Elizabeth Fry had become something of a role model for her in terms of how she envisioned her historic six decades of service as Brittain's prime regent.

As a result of Elizabeth's larger efforts, prison standards throughout the United Kingdom were transformed. Women's privacy was protected from men, women replaced men as supervisors of women, children and adults began learning to read, clothing and other necessities were provided for women and children, payment was made to prisoners doing work, and Bibles and sewing materials were made available to women in prison. This allowed female prisoners to make meaningful use of their time, and women were enabled to earn money, furthering the improvement of their situations in prison. Overall, it also led to a philosophical change in the British penal system. Prisons are not for degradation but for reform. Further, prisoners have rights as human beings, and prisons are responsible for their care and wellbeing while under their custody. As her work influenced prison reform societies to be developed across the United Kingdom and in Russia, Prussia, the United States, France, Italy, Switzerland, and the Netherlands, her contribution was also organizational. In 1827, Elizabeth published her own report on the conditions and governance of female prisons, in which she concludes:

> Much depends on the spirit in which the visiter [sic] enters upon her work. It must be the spirit, not of judgment, but of mercy. She must not say in her heart, *I am more holy than thou*; but must rather keep in perpetual remembrance that 'all have sinned, and come short of the glory of God'—that, therefore, great pity is due from us, even to the greatest transgressors among our fellow-creatures—and that in meekness and love, we ought to labour for their restoration. (Fry, 1827, pp. 20-21)

Convict Ships to Australia and Restoration Concerns

Early on, Elizabeth Fry became aware of rioting within the prison at a particular time in the year when several hundred women would be rounded up, paraded through the city, and sent to Australia. On the way to the *convict ships*, however, they suffered humiliation and sometimes injury, as London crowds hurled garbage and refuse at them, shouting derision on their way to the docks. Upon learning about these spectacles, Elizabeth stepped in, bringing about change and hope. First, she insisted on the transport be conducted in closed carriages instead of open wagons. This would protect the women from insults and injury. Second, she rode with them as a statement of solidarity. Third, she convinced ship captains to free the women from their chains and shackles for the sake of their health and wellbeing. One woman had screamed in pain as the blacksmith blasted loose the rivets holding the clasps together, which by now had broken the skin, causing infection. Fourth, women were divided into groups of six so they could be assured a place at table, and they were divided into classes of twelve, with a female matron appointed as overseer (versus male guards that too often took advantage of women). These measures allowed their educational and social support networks to be maintained. Fifth, she organized the provision of each woman with a large bag of supplies that would allow women to do something productive with their time on the long journey.

Organized by the *British Ladies Society for Promoting the Reformation of Female Prisoners Convict Ship sub-committee*, this work made a huge difference in the lives of these women. With fabric contributions from Manchester textile mills and financial support from various donors, the "bag of useful things" each woman was given contained:

> One Bible, one Hessian apron, one black stuff ditto, one black cotton cap, one large Hessian bag, one small bag containing a piece of tape, an ounce of pins, one hundred needles, four balls of white sewing cotton, one ditto black, one ditto blue, one ditto red, two balls of black worsted, twenty-four hanks of coloured thread, one cloth with eight darning needles, one small bodkin fastened on it; two stay-laces, one thimble, one pair of scissors, one pair of spectacles when required, one comb, one small ditto, knife and fork, and a ball of string. (Bardens, 2004, pp. 52-53)

Not only did such provisions make the 4-6-month journey more manageable, but they also furthered the likelihood that women might thereby earn a bit of money and even find employment rather than being sold into sex-slavery or the like. The ratio of convict men transferred to women in Australia was nine to one, and women were described as "tamers and breeders," intended to build a new society. As many as one fifth of Australia's population descends from one of these transferred convict women. One of the stops along the way was Rio de Janeiro, and women could sell a quilt there in order to have some money by the time they reached their destination. They could also sell their work in Australia or at Botany Bay in Tasmania, the two primary destinations of the convict ships. Only one of these quilts is still in existence: the *Rajah Quilt* (named after the ship on which it was made in 1841), which was created on the way from Woolrich to Hobart and is now on display at the National Gallery of Australia. It bears marks of small bloodstains, perhaps signaling the work of women sewing with sharp needles on the rough, high seas.

Between 1788 and 1868, as many as 25,000 women were sent abroad so as to alleviate overcrowding in prisons and to establish a British colony down under, and nearly half of them (just under 12,000) were ministered to by Elizabeth Fry and her companions between 1818 and 1843. She visited 106 transport ships, missing only one departure over that quarter century. Her work also bolstered a movement toward the eventual abolition of transportation. By the time women arrived in Australia or Tasmania, if they had acquired sewing or embroidery skills and were able to read, their lots would likely have been improved. In Australia and Tasmania, some eleven female factories or houses of correction for female convicts were built. This allowed women to contribute profitably over an indentured period of service, sometimes lasting ten years. The one surviving facility, the *Cascades Female Factory* in South Hobart, Tasmania, was built in 1828, serving until 1856, as the transportation of convicts had waned. In these factories, women spun linen and wool, wove textiles, did laundry, cleaned ropes, and performed other menial tasks. Preserved now as a World Heritage site (as of 2010), the humane values of Elizabeth Fry are evident in the layout of quarters, gathering places, and work rooms.

In addition to caring for women prisoners, Elizabeth Fry was also concerned about people's reformation and restoration to society as upstanding contributors. The *Rheinish-Westfalian Prison Society*, organized by Theodor Fliedner, had not only benefited from the advances made at Newgate, but they had also advanced programs aimed at the prevention of crime and the reduction of recidivism, or backsliding (Jorns, 1933, pp. 194-95). As a concern for women just released from prison having a place to land, Elizabeth opened a home called *Tothill Fields Asylum* for nurture and support. It later became known as a *Refuge* for the young offender in Westminster, and in 1840, Queen Victoria donated £50 in support of the project after Elizabeth was invited to meet with the Queen. Queen Victoria described Elizabeth as a "very superior person," and to some degree, her balancing of family, leadership, and social concerns followed the trail that Elizabeth had blazed.

In November of 1828, Joseph's W. S. & Fry's Bank went bankrupt, and Joseph John Gurney took over the financial interests of the family, paying off their debts. He also supported Elizabeth's charitable work, including caring for the homeless in London. As a result of business failure, though, Joseph was disowned by Barking Friends Meeting, though he was reinstated a decade later. The Friends testimony regarding business integrity was perceived to have been breeched, and the Fry family received criticism from Friends and others, as well as admiration. Anglican clergyman Sydney Smith felt that offering prisoners meaningful work was not an effective deterrent to crime, and Elizabeth was accused of mollycoddling criminals. Still others were intimidated by her exemplary work, as it made other persons of faith look dilatory in their inaction. "She is very unpopular with the clergy," wrote the Reverend Sydney Smith, wryly in 1821, "examples of living, active virtue disturb our response and give birth to distressing comparisons. We long to burn her alive." (Blythe, 2000, p. 257)

Elizabeth's virtue and compassion thus received condemnation for opposite reasons, for failures and successes alike. In an address to Parliament, Lord Sidmouth warned that Fry and other reformers were dangerous people, as they were trying to "remove the dread of punishment in the criminal classes." His successor, however, Sir Robert Peel, was more sympathetic to her work. Because of her influence, *the Gaol's Act of 1823* was passed, which insured the supervision of women prisoners by female personnel. It also called for the classification of women prisoners, so that those simply awaiting trial or imprisoned for minor offenses were not housed with those convicted of more serious crimes, such as murder or violence. It provided for the education of women and their children in prisons, and it made it possible for women to do work that was compensated so that they could improve their lot while in prison.

The Institution for Nursing Sisters and Other Concerns

In addition to working to transform prison systems and reforming systems worldwide, Elizabeth Fry also championed other concerns. Impressed by the nursing work that Catholic Sisters of Charity and the Institute of Deaconesses in Kaiserswerth, Germany had developed, in 1840 Elizabeth Fry founded the *Institution of Nursing Sisters* in London. This contributed to the establishment of nursing as a profession in Britain. Beginning with a training school for nurses in Guy's Hospital, the "Fry nurses" wore brown uniforms and cared for patients' spiritual needs as well as their physical ones. The Institution of Nursing Sisters was based at Devonshire Square from 1842-1860, and while she remained its president until her death in 1845, it was also supported by her brother Samuel's wife Elizabeth Gurney, sister in-law Elizabeth Gurney, her daughters, and other women.

Again, the goal of the Institution was to glorify God and to mitigate human suffering. Put missionally, "It is the spirit of the Institution of Nursing Sisters that the poor should be attended in their houses with the same kindness and care bestowed upon the more wealthy part of the community." That being the case, Elizabeth believed that the poor needed medical care—sometimes in their own homes—just as much as the rich, who could afford hospital care. While much of the Institution's work was self-sustaining, the Queen Dowager Adelaide became a patron of the work, supporting it financially. As a result of these advances, other Protestant nursing sisterhoods began to emerge, and Florence Nightingale (a relative of Elizabeth's) was influenced by her views on the training of nurses. Elizabeth Fry's Institution for Nursing Sisters thus bolstered the development of Florence Nightingale's training program, and some Fry Nurses went with Nightingale to Crimea, as they cared for wounded soldiers in 1854. In that sense, Elizabeth Fry deserves to be called "the founder of nursing" in the English-speaking world, in addition to her many other achievements (Huntsman, Bruin, & Holttum, 2002).

Overall, the lifetime contributions of Elizabeth Fry were ordered by her call to ministry and serving the needs of humanity in every aspect of her life, her willingness to get involved and commit personally, and her ability to establish organizations that would expand the work collectively and continue it institutionally beyond her personal influence. Along these lines, note a number of additional organizations that she established.

- After seeing the body of a boy who had frozen to death, she established a *Nightly Shelter* in London in 1820.
- Having moving to the seaside for fresh air at Brighton for health reasons in 1824, she found extensive poverty and set up the *Brighton District Visiting Society*—the first of many *Visiting Societies* throughout the United Kingdom as a local approach to addressing issues of poverty, hunger, education, and homelessness.
- To improve the perennial problem of relations between servants and mistresses, she founded a *Servants' Society* in 1825.
- Because of her lifelong friendship with Amelia Opie, whose family were active in the movement for *universal suffrage*, Elizabeth also gave her support to developing *associations for women's rights*.
- Having encountered a member of the Coast Guard who struggled under the burden of their assignments, Elizabeth worked to establish *libraries*

for Coast Guard stations around the United Kingdom, and by 1836, over 500 Coast Guard libraries were established, providing also bases for education in remote locations.

- In 1840, Elizabeth attended the *World Anti-Slavery Convention* at Exeter Hall, and she worked with Clarkson, Wilberforce, and Buxton for the abolition of slavery, hosting also a *summer anti-slavery meeting* at her home in 1843.

Elizabeth and Joseph moved to a smaller house in 1829 to reduce expenses—The Cedars on Upton Lane. In the last months of her life, Elizabeth moved to the coast, and on October 13, 1845, she suffered a stroke and died at Ramsgate. She was laid to rest at the Quaker burial-ground in Barking with more than a thousand mourners in silent attendance. In recent years, her gravestone was moved to Stansted Meeting's burial grounds, a few miles north. Following her death, an asylum to perpetuate her memory was commissioned by the Lord Mayor of London, and the *Elizabeth Fry Refuge* for released female prisoners was established in 1849. Upon her death, the Seamen of the Ramsgate Coast Guard flew their flag at half-mast honoring her legacy, a practice until that time reserved for the death of a ruling monarch. A marble statue of Elizabeth Fry was erected at the Old Bailey courthouse in 1907.

The Legacy of Elizabeth Fry

The legacy of Elizabeth Fry was historic and extensive, and yet, she did not escape criticism. Some questioned her investing time and energies outside the home instead of caring more fully for her children. Several of her children were educated in boarding schools or in Norwich, living with other family members. Nonetheless, her children supported her work, although none of them remained within the Society of Friends throughout their lifetimes, tending to marry out of meeting. Others questioned whether the Fry Bank's bankruptcy was caused by supporting her charitable causes, but economic collapses in Britain and Europe are more realistically to blame. Nonetheless, her calling to ministry indeed took her in a great number of world-changing directions. Not only did she see a regular reading of the New Testament as key to personal and social transformation, but in her social work, she was indeed translating the New Testament in world-changing ways.

So, what was the key to her success? Her daughter Katharine described it as "her dignified and stately presence, her exquisite voice, and her constant and unruffled sweetness of expression—the same to crowned heads and to prisoners" (Richards, 1916, p. 108). The Scottish Duke of Argyll declares that "She was the only really very great human being I have ever met with whom it was impossible to be disappointed. She was, in the fullest sense of the word, a majestic woman." The Prussian ambassador called her his "favourite saint" (Whitney, 1937, pp. 291-304) and her brother, Joseph John Gurney, says of her,

> The law of love, which might be said to be ever on her lips, was deeply engraved on her heart; and her charity, in the best and most comprehensive sense of the term, flowed freely forth towards her fellow-men of every class, of every condition. Thus with a peculiar grace she won her way, and almost uniformly obtained her object.... This perseverance was combined with a peculiar versatility and readiness for seizing on every passing occasion, and converting it into an opportunity of usefulness. She was not only always willing, but always prepared, always ready (by a kind of mental sleight of hand) to do good, be it ever so little, to a child, a servant, a waiter at an inn, a friend, a neighbour, a stranger! (Timpson, 1847, pp. 274-75)

In addition to her personal and spontaneous responsiveness to human need, an overall basis for her historic impact was her organizational and administrative prowess. Not only did she become involved personally with addressing human needs, she organized dozens of associations and societies that sustained the work long after her personal involvement was completed. By proper stewardship of her elevated place in society and her connectedness to Friends, she furthered her concerns corporately, including the campaigning for changes in operating procedures and legal standards.

While Elizabeth Fry effectively campaigned for prison reforms throughout Britain and Europe, she also contributed to many additional institutional changes in the long term—establishing and furthering schools, nursing training programs, slavery abolition, Bible associations, libraries, shelters, and other venues of addressing social concerns. In honor of her legacy, the Elizabeth Fry Society was established in Vancouver, Canada in 1939, and a larger Association expanded that work three decades later. Her image was selected to grace the £5 note between 2002 and 2016, when it was replaced by that of Winston Churchill. In addition to being referenced as "the angel of the prisons," Elizabeth Fry was also indeed, *a Quaker of note!*

Discussion Questions

1. In reflecting upon the formative years of Elizabeth Gurney Fry, how did her early spiritual experiences lead to a sense of vocation and a call to ministry, to which she sought to be faithful the rest of her life?

2. How did the regular practice of Bible reading within the life of the Gurney and Fry families lead later to Elizabeth's conviction that public Bible reading would be a formative force for personal transformation, moral guidance, and societal reform in her prison work and educational endeavors?

3. How did Elizabeth Fry's experiences with people who were suffering convince her that something needed to be done to address pressing social concerns, and how did she endeavor to establish organizational and institutional means of addressing those concerns long term, beyond the time-bound contributions of a single individual?

4. How does Elizabeth Fry serve as an inspiring example for others to follow in addressing the social and justice concerns of later generations, despite the challenges faced in every situation?

References

Bardens, D. (2004). *Elizabeth Fry: Britain's second lady on the five-pound note.* Chanadon.

Bayne, A. (1869). *A comprehensive history of Norwich.* Jarrold and Sons.

Blythe, R. (2000). *Out of the Valley: Another Year at Wormingwood.* Viking.

Cooper, R., A. (1979). The English Quakers and prison reform 1809-23. *Quaker History* 68 (1), 3-19.

Craig, R., L. (2006). Women in corrections: Elizabeth Gurney Fry. *The Journal of Correctional Education,* 57(2), 141-44.

Crone, R. (2017). Elizabeth Fry: The great reformer. *BBC History Magazine.* 44-47.

Fry, E. (n.d). *What Owest Thou unto Thy Lord?* [Sermon]. http://www.qhpress.org/quakerpages/qhoa/fryserm.htm.

Fry, E., G. (1827). *Observations on the visiting, superintendence and government of female prisoners.* J. and A. Arch.

Fry, K., & Cresswell, E. (1974). *Memoir of the life of Elizabeth Fry with extracts from her journal and letters* (Vol. 2). Patterson Smith.

Garland, H., A. (1869). *The life of John Randolph of Roanoke* (Vol. 2). Haskell House Publishers Ltd.

Gurney, J., J. (1819). *Notes on visits made to some of the prisons in Scotland and the north of England, in company with Elizabeth Fry.* A. Constable and Co.

Hale, Sarah J. (1842). Editor's Table. *Godey's Lady's book, and ladies' American magazine* 24-25, 304-06.

Howard, J. (1777). *The state of prisons in England and Wales: With preliminary observations, and an account of some foreign prisons.* William Eyres.

Hugh, B. (1985). *Slavery and theology: writings of seven Quaker reformers, 1800-1870* (B. Hugh, Ed.). Prinit Press.

Huntsman, R. G., Bruin, M. & Holttum, D. (2002). Twixt candle and lamp: the contribution of Elizabeth Fry and the nursing sisters to nursing reform. *Medical History,* 46, 351-80.

Isba, A. (2010). *The excellent Mrs. Fry: Unlikely heroine.* Continuum.

Jorns, A. (1933). *Prison reform, the Quakers as pioneers in social work* (T. K. Brown, Trans.). *Kennika.*

Jowett, C. (2017). *The history of Newgate prison.* Pen & Sword History.

Larsen, T. (2011). *People of one book: The Bible and the Victorians.* Oxford University Press.

Larsen, T. (2013). *The Bible and varieties of nineteenth-century dissent—Elizabeth Fry, Mary Carpenter, and Catherine Booth. Dissent and the Bible in Britain, 1650-1950.* Oxford University Press.

Leng, F. (2006). *Invincible spirits: a thousand years of women's spiritual writings.* Eerdmans.

Martin, R., H. (1996). Quakers, the Bible, and the British and foreign Bible society. *Quaker History,* 85, 13-28.

Richards, L., E. (1916). *Elizabeth Fry: the angel of the prisons.* D. Appleton and Company.

Rose, J. (1980). *Elizabeth Fry.* St. Martin's Press.

Savery, W. (1861). *A journal of the life, travels, and religious labors of William Savery.* Stereotype.

Schrock, A., A. (2016). To act in the spirit not of judgment, but of mercy. *Christian History,* 117, 29-32.

Steward, L. (1993). *Women volunteer to go to prison: a history of the Elizabeth Fry society of British Columbia.* Orca Publishers.

Swiss, D., J. (2010). *The tin ticket: the heroic journey of Australia's convict women.* Berkley.

Timpson, T. (1847). *Memoirs of Elizabeth Fry.* Aylott and Jones.

Whitney, J. (1972). *Elizabeth Fry: Quaker heroine.* Benjamin Blom, Inc.

5 | Lucretia Mott
Imagination, Empathy and Grief

By Mark Bredin

According to Margaret Bacon, Lucretia "lacked a soaring imagination but she had the gift of empathy; she could easily put herself in the place of another and feel his or her pain or joy" (Bacon, 1980, p. 22). Carol Faulkner states that she was an extrovert who loved to be involved and surrounded by people (Faulkner, 2011, p. 6). Susan Lanzoni, observes that Jung believed "the penchant for empathy made one an extrovert…" (Lanzoni, 2018, p. 69). To embrace empathy, in other words, is to imagine oneself *as* another (Brueggemann, 1993, p. 16 & Rollins, 2013, pp. 105-111).

I propose that Lucretia was a woman of imagination. Michael Birkel comments that "Imagination opens the way to perceiving how those who bear the burden of injustice feel" (Birkel, 2003, p. 20). *Lucretia amplified her imagination to embrace the burdens of the oppressed and oppressor alike as her own through self-reflection and meditation on the Bible.* I suggest that Lucretia's criticism of slavery and injustice begins with her capacity for empathy and grief. I show that she found in the Bible, particularly, in Jeremiah and Jesus, this capacity of empathy and grief to be manifest energizing people to imagine something beyond the accepted given. Jeremiah and Jesus provided an inspiration to cry out against the injustices, calling people, from their lethargy, to see the innocent blood on their hands, and to imagine something beyond this apathy.

At Marlboro Chapel in 1841 she calls for empathy, grief, and imagination to seek justice:

Who can look at the crimes and sufferings of men, and not labor for reformation? Let us put our own souls in their souls' stead, who are in slavery, and let us labor for their liberation as bound with them. Let us look at the souls who are led away into hopeless captivity, deprived of every right, and sundered from every happy association... (Densmore, 2017, p. 11).

In her *Discourse on Woman* in 1849 she refers to the Bible as calling "forth the benevolent affections and higher nature" (Densmore, 2017, p. 73). This higher nature evokes empathy and grief for the oppressed and oppressor and energizes the hope for alternatives.

The Elite and Imagination

Why does Bacon claim Lucretia lacked imagination? In her address at Marlboro Chapel in 1841 she says:

> I am aware that the imaginations of many have become so depraved, and their minds so enervated, by appeals to the passions and the imagination, from the inferior literature of the novelist, that it needs not only strong effort to arouse them from lethargy in which they live, to true and noble activity: but a tender care is needed to preserve them from the evils consequent upon their long inactivity (Densmore, 2017, p. 10).

Lucretia's words "but tender care is needed" reveal her strong empathy for her audience as she grieves for their depraved imaginations that prevented embracing empathy.

Lucretia distinguishes between "imagination" that leads to "true and noble activity" and "imagination" designed by the elites to maintain their privileges. In 1849 addressing medical students, she refers to the "works of imagination" such as the theatre, ball room, "the sickly and sentimental novel and pernicious romance" as "stimulating drinks when long indulged in, enervate the mind, unfitting it for sober duties of life" (Densmore, 2017, p. 73).[1] Such activities prevented the embrace of empathy and grief for the oppressed and numbed them from their own culpability in such oppression.

At Cherry Street Meeting[2] in 1850 she laments the propaganda to numb people's sense of the evil of slavery:

---

[1] Densmore, (2017, p. 115): At the women's rights convention at Cleveland in 1853, she speaks of "sickly sentimental yellow-covered literature" that women read; she concludes that in such reading "we cannot expect that she will be much."

[2] This is her own meeting house for worship.

There is now going the rounds of the papers an address which will produce a most baneful influence upon society, on the great subject of humanity, slavery, tending to direct the mind to it as a kind of providential
thing, and scarcely admitting it to be an evil (Densmore, 2017, p. 86).

The elites controlled the imaginations of society through poetry, epic, sacred music, tragedy, comedy, erotic verse, and history.[3] They provided escape for people
distancing them from the poor and oppressed. They cover the truth that civilized
culture is rooted in violence, selfishness, and greed.

Lucretia consistently attacks the ecclesiastical elites for their misuse of
the Bible to justify slavery and subjugation of women, and war. She comments
that "the Bible has been quoted to authorize nearly every wrong in which people
have been found" (Densmore, 2017, p. 21). At the Unitarian Church in 1843, she
comments: "the Bible is ill-used… Instead of taking the truths of the Bible in
corroboration of the right, the practice has been, to turn over its pages to find
example and authority for the wrong, for the existing abuses of society"
(Densmore, 2017, p. 113). At Marlboro Chapel in 1841 she asks: has not "the
priest-craft and monopoly of the pulpit…long held women bound?" (Densmore,
2017, p. 9).

The Prophetic Imagination

The unconscious is the repository of the true imagination, from which
fantasies, visions of the future, new ideas, and insights emerge (Rollins, 2013, p.
103). A person of prophetic imagination, according to Brueggemann, draws
from the unconscious content (Brueggemann, 2001, p. xiv). At the center of the
unconscious is God's dwelling presence. Walter Wink calls it the "transcendent
dimension to conscience that is not socialized, but that represents the ineradica-
ble image of God within us" (Wink, 2002, p. 72). Jung and his followers call this
presence the Self. Rollins comments on the drive of the Self to integrate with the
conscious in terms of *being-in-relationship*:

A definitive characteristic of the Self is its sense of being *in relation*, both
with others and with the historical-cultural stream of which we are part.
"Coming to one's Self," Jung maintains, involves a simultaneous coming to conscious acknowledgment and acceptance of our kinship with
those around us. Because relationship to the self is at once relationship
to our fell man… (Rollins, 2013, p. 38).

---

[3] Faulkner, 2011, p. 93 notes Lucretia's dislike of the higher cultures of English society in her
visit in 1840.

Being in touch *with* and accessing this treasury of imagination is important because it is, as Wink points out, separate from society and its values that perpetuated domination of the elite; "it is something of God within us" (Wink, 2002, p. 72).

Brueggemann writes: "The task of prophetic imagination is to cut through the numbness, to penetrate the self-deception..." (Brueggemann, 200, p. 45) noting that "*prophetic* must be *imaginative* because it is urgently out beyond the ordinary and the reasonable" (Brueggemann, 2001, p. xv). Brueggemann argues that it is beyond the ordinary and the reasonable because our consciousness is so dominated by the elites that we cannot imagine other than what they tell us. It is hard to imagine a society rooted in "acceptance of our kinship with those around us;" in fact it is hard to hear and see the suffering and pain of others.

Brueggemann identifies key attributes of the prophetic imagination to be that of grieving and empathy for the oppressed and oppressor (Brueggemann, 2001, p. 51). He sees Jeremiah as the clearest model for prophetic imagination. He notes the grief of Jeremiah at two levels: (1) he grieved and cared about the oppressed and oppressor because of his sense of God's care; (2) he grieved because no one would listen and no one would see what was so transparent to him (Brueggemann, 2001, p. 47).

Lisa Vetter comments on the inner-light in reference to Lucretia: "The 'inner-light' emerges when human beings engage in quiet reflection... The 'inner-light' may also emerge when people engage in good acts such as advocating for equality and justice for all people" (Vetter, 2015, p. 606). Lucretia called for all to have "a portion of every day of the week, for mental and spiritual improvement" (Densmore, 2017, p. 33) as a way of being in touch with the imagination within the unconscious, i.e., so that the inner-light imagination emerges. Lucretia's strong empathy and preference for prophetic texts left her open to embrace the prophetic imagination that emerges from the inner-light. Lucretia transcends the elite's consciousness and articulates the utterings of the inner-light expressed in her heart-felt empathy for her society. Lucretia challenges medical students to make "opportunities for meditation and reflection" and "be led to reflect upon your duties, and responsibility of your position in society" (Densmore, 2017, p. 53). She pleads: "...they be willing to receive that which conflicts with their education, their prejudices and preconceived opinions" (Densmore, 2017, p. 53).

At the Unitarian Church in 1843 she encourages her audience to imagine a life *as* other than dominated by elite consciousness through empathy, sympathy, and grief for the conditions of the oppressed:

> Oh have your minds cultivated and your hearts enlightened, hesitate not
> to speak of the evils which surround you – it may be unpopular for a

time, but it is diffusing itself over the nation, and I rejoice that the time may come when violence and war will cease to crimson the land… We should remember the poor, call in to see them in their abodes of want and distress; call not in to see your rich acquaintances in preference to those who are objects of compassion and charity – it is to the poor, the maimed and the blind, that we are to administer (Densmore, 2017, p. 25).

Brueggemann states that "It is the vocation of the prophet to keep alive the ministry of imagination, to keep on conjuring and proposing futures alternative to the single one the king wants to urge as the only thinkable one" (Brueggemann, 2001, p. 40). Further he writes: "The prophet is engaged in a battle for language, in an effort to create a different epistemology out of which another community might emerge" (Brueggemann, 2001, p. 55). Lucretia lived to keep alive the prophetic imagination through self-reflection, grieving and embracing empathy for the world and its suffering, evoked by the Bible's teaching's about justice and equality.

Jeremiah and Jesus
In this final section I examine briefly the influence of Jeremiah and Jesus on Lucretia.

Jeremiah
In worship at Cherry Street Meeting in 1850 Lucretia begins her sermon quoting twenty-four lines of poetry by Isaac Watts (Densmore, 2017, p. 82). She perceived this poem to impede prophetic imagination as it presented poverty and oppression as God's divine providence. This led people, according to Lucretia, to detach themselves from the poor and oppressed, i.e. being un-empathetic and unmoved. Lucretia engages critically and mournfully with a poem arising from Watts' elite consciousness. Her goal is to engage the depraved and numb imaginations of her listeners and bring them to imagine empathetically.

Lucretia challenges them:

> Let not our religion be directed into a strain which shall lead us into less sympathy for suffering and erring humanity, and let mercy, which must be coupled with justice and love, influence us, and we shall be instrumental in relieving the afflicted mourners in Zion (Densmore, 2017, p. 85)

Lucretia notes the importance here of embracing empathy for suffering society in contrast to Watts' poem that numbs people's natural emotions to the oppressed and poor. Lucretia is moved by Jeremiah as one who suffered with the oppressed. She particularly alludes to Lamentations 1:16 and 3:55 proclaiming:

> We may, with the mourning Prophet Jeremiah, have a right to say "Mine eyes are running down with water because the comforter that should relieve my soul is far from me." Again we adopt his language, and return multiplied blessings and thanksgivings because "that when I was in the low dungeon thou heardest me" (Densmore, 2017, p 86)

Lucretia ponders in her meditations on the suffering of slaves and the need to empathize with them that must involve "mourning." She says: "We need to learn the true Christianity that will lead us to put our souls in the souls' stead of the oppressed" (Densmore, 2017, p. 86). Jeremiah indeed experiences their suffering as his own and grieves for it. She could not separate his grief from the suffering of God's chosen people in exile. She too imagined herself in the dungeon. She laments:

> Oh! that there were hearts to so feel for these suffering and dumb, as to cry aloud and spare not, showing unto this nation its transgression… If this were the case we should not see and hear and read of the efforts that are made to sustain this giant, monstrous evil. We should rather be led to look at our own garments, to see how far they were cleansed from participation in its iniquities; to feel that we must not build our house by unrighteousness, nor our chambers by wrong, we must not use our neighbor's services with wages and give him not for he work. (Densmore, 2017, p. 86)

Lucretia also engages empathetically with Jeremiah 22:13 when she comments about not building "our house by unrighteousness" and regarding unpaid wages (cf. James 5:4). The sense of grief and embrace of empathy is at the heart of Lucretia's prophetic criticizing of the elite consciousness exemplified in Watts' poem. Lucretia surely inspired by Jeremiah calls people to examine their lives and their culpability in oppression. Brueggemann comments that "he [Jeremiah] does this to penetrate the numb denial of the royal community, which pretended things must go on forever" (Brueggemann, 2001, p. 115). Similarly Lucretia in her empathy and grieving for the poor seeks to penetrate the elite's imaginations. In her sermon she is so immersed and in empathy with Jeremiah 22:13 that she is able to add to Jeremiah when she challenges herself and her listeners to "be led to look at our garments, to see how far they were cleansed from participation in its iniquities." Lucretia here has in mind the dilemma she and her husband James had regarding using materials that had involved slavery.

Jesus

At the American Anti-Slavery Society in 1848 we find an empathetic approach to Jesus' Sermon on the Mount by Lucretia:

> Ye have head that it was said by them of old, thou shalt treat thy slaves kindly, thou shalt prepare them for freedom at a *future* day; but I say unto you hold no slaves at all, proclaim liberty now throughout the land to all the inhabitants thereof." Let this be the loud sounding jubilee that shall be uttered. Let us no longer be blinded by the dim theology that only in the far seeing vision discovers a millennium, when violence shall no more be heard in the land – wasting nor destruction in her borders; but let us behold it now, nigh at the door – lending faith and confidence to our hopes, assuring us that even we ourselves shall be instrumental in proclaiming liberty to the captive (Densmore, 2017 p. 42).

Zulick and Leff comment on Lucretia's use of the gospels:

> A simultaneous identification and transfer of authority is performed between the passive older order: *it was said*; and the new, active rhetorical subject: *but I say*. This constituted a radical transmutation from traditional to charismatic authority in the Gospels; and, of course, when Coffin Mott reproduces it, she is placing the reformer in the slot formerly occupied by Christ (Zulick and Leff, 1995, p. 28).

Ann Ryan writes: "She [Mott] did what Jesus himself had done and went beyond the words of scripture in order to be faithful to the spirit" (Ryan, 2000, p. 293). In Lucretia's adaption of Jesus' words, it is important again to see her concern to challenge numb imaginations "blinded by the dim theology…." Lucretia imagines Jesus on the mount speaking with feeling and empathy for the oppressed, but intensifying traditional teaching with the spirit of God present within.

Conclusion

Christopher Bryant emphasizes the imagination in the battle against secular hedonism:

> The…chief weapon against the soporific influences of our secularized culture is imagination exercised in the service of faith. For it is secularized imagination fed by televised advertisements and the other mass media which hypnotizes us with the illusion that a good time in this

world is all that matters – despite the constantly experienced truth that the more you seek pleasure the more it eludes you. But the secularized imagination needs to be countered by a believing imagination (Bryant, 1987, p. 18).

Lisa Vetter observes that Lucretia "continually exhorts her audience to engage in intensive self-reflection to be alert to subtle incidences of coercion" (Vetter, 2015, p. 622). Vetter sees Lucretia as one who countered the coercive effects of the "secularized imagination." Lucretia's starting point of action is to experience grief and empathy for the oppressed and the oppressor as energized by the prophetic imagination. Reading the prophets stirred that of God's presence within that corroborated her sense of what is right and wrong. Her sense of the prophetic imagination sensitized her to see the elite's coercion to anaesthetize people's imaginations.

Discussion Question

Ponder on what you mean by empathy; discuss its meaning in terms of social work and activism; consider how the elite consciousness might lead you to lack empathy and what consequences that might have on your work for social reformation; think about being a social worker with fading empathy, leaving you neither with grief nor anger against injustice. In the light of this ask: How seriously do you take Lucretia's invitation to self-reflect to activate the imagination?

References

Bacon, M.H. (1980). *Valiant Friend: The Life of Lucretia Mott.* (New York: Walker and Company).

Birkel, M. (2003). A Near Sympathy: The Timeless Quaker Wisdom of John Woolman. *(Richmond, Indiana: Friends United Press)*.

Brueggemann, W. (1993). The Bible and Postmodern Imagination: Texts under Negotiation. *(London: SCM)*.

Brueggemann, W. (2001). The Prophetic Imagination. *(Second Edition. Minneapolis: Fortress Press)*.

Bryant, C. (1987). Journey to the Centre: Explorations in the Realm of the Spirit. *(London: Darton, Longman and Todd)*.

Densmore, C., C. Faulkner, N. Hewitt, B. W. Palmer (eds.) (2017). Lucretia Mott Speaks: The Essential Speeches and Sermons. *(Urbana, Chicago, and Springfield: University of Illinois Press.*

Faulkner, C. (2017). Lucretia Mott's Heresy: Abolition and Women's Rights in Nineteenth-Century America. *(Philadelphia: University of Pennsylvania Press)*.

Lanzoni, S. (2018). Empathy: A History. (*New Haven and London: Yale University Press*).

Rollins, W. G. (2013). Jung and the Bible. *(Eugene, Oregon: WIPF & STOCK.*

Ryan, A. (2000). Nothing 'too sacred to question': The spirituality of Lucretia Mott. (*Graduate Theological Union.* Unpublished PhD).

Vetter, L. (2015). The most belligerent non-resistant: Lucretia Mott on women's rights. *Political Theory.* 43(5): pp. 600-630.

Wink, W. (2002). The Human Being: Jesus and the Enigma of the Son of the Man. (Minneapolis Fortress Press).

Zulick, M., & M. Leff, (1995). "Time and the True Light" in Lucretia Mott's 'Discourse on Woman.'" *Rhetoric Society Quarterly* 25, Annual Issue (1995): pp. 20-31.

6 | <u>WWJAD</u>
The Transformation of Jane Addams Quaker Beginnings into Burgeoning Social Work Values: Are Community Challenges Different Today & What <u>W</u>ould <u>J</u>ane <u>A</u>ddams <u>D</u>o?

By Wendy Grab

Jane Addams' "contributions to American society in the early twentieth century were immeasurable. As a pacifist, social worker, suffragist, political activist, educator, community organizer, and defender of immigrants and the poor, she challenged the status quo in a way that altered American conceptions of social justice" (Ruttum, 2011, p.105).

Today's profession of social work has deeply held values that center around service, standing up for human rights and for social justice throughout all the different levels of social work practice. There are six identified core values within the Social Work Code of Ethics. These core values would look very different today if not for Jane Addams' great works. Her contributions to the field were integral not only to the creation of the social work profession itself but to the underpinnings of its most basic tenets. When one delves into these foundational values it becomes clear that they are intertwined with testimonials from Jane's unique Quaker upbringing. In order for this exploration of the relationship between social work and Quaker values to be relatable to those not familiar with Quakerism I chose to use the shortened SPICES testimonials, as they appear to be utilized in many Quaker schools to help teach these important foundations. These interlaced values continue to thrive today as in Jane's time and support the major works and the Grand Challenges for Social Work initiatives that are the focus of today's profession.

Simplicity

Arranging life so the inner light is unobstructed/clearing the way for what is important ("Quaker Values", n.d.)

Service

Elevate service to others above self-interest ("Read the Code," n.d.)

Being raised in a household that truly emulated many deeply held Quaker values created a unique opportunity for young Jane Addams to become quite the renaissance woman.

Klosterman and Stratton describe how she "admired her father's Quaker tendencies of courage, moral integrity, and belief that shared values transcend differences, such as nationality, creed, or race" (2006, p.158). From these humble beginnings she grew to have great compassion for the poor and the oppressed. She felt called to serve those in need who lacked a voice of their own. The openness of Quakers supporting alternative roles for women undoubtedly set Jane free to engage in her social service work rather than accepting the traditional gender roles of her time. Without this foundation Jane may not have had such an important role in social justice, peace, women's suffrage, and social work (Mays, 2004). She lived a life of service, and as such started many social service programs to meet the needs of her community (Molkup, 1972). Much of Jane's work continues today through several fields in the social sciences, human services, various foundations, state and federal legislature, aid programming, peace movements, and more.

The Hull House Settlement was the touchstone that opened the way for Jane to become involved in multiple areas of human need, social justice challenges, community programming, and peace efforts. The settlement had a robust connection with various religious groups, especially Quakers, and embraced similar beliefs in many instances. Addams incorporated many of these beliefs and practices into her community and global concerns, as well as her social activism (Besthorn, 2002). She passionately believed in and practiced cultural humility/diversity, inclusion, and equality for all (Klosterman & Stratton, 2006). She embraced the heritage of all those in the community and purported celebrating cultural differences rather than pushing for cultural assimilation (Lundblad, 1995). She was sincerely "concerned for the quality of life of her neighbors. She invited them into Hull-House as she would have invited them into her own home" (Molkup, 1972, p.3).

Jane became a trailblazer for many professions and was a lifelong advocate for many social causes both in the United States and across the world. Some of her biggest impacts were in the field of social work, community organizing, and the juvenile justice system. Known as the "mother of social work" she sincerely embodied her father's handed down Quaker values and weaved them into all of her good works. She was known internationally as a purveyor of peace, social justice, and international aid (Klosterman & Stratton, 2006). Jane's self-lessness and compassion were reminisced about through her neighbors "who remembered her warmth and always loving kindness, her willingness to listen and, if necessary, to act at any hour of the day or night, her complete and un-shakable belief in the worth of the human person, no matter how outrageous his words or unpleasant his deeds" (Kendall, 1962, p.84).

There are quite a few connections between Social Work's cardinal val-ues and Quaker testimonial values. One can see this connection in how Jane valued all individuals and sought out their strengths and the gifts/talents of their communities. This opened the way for much of her empowerment work and social justice callings (Klosterman & Stratton, 2006). She authentically reflected Quaker principles in her Social Work activities through her ardent advocacy sup-porting equality for all people regardless of their background, gender, beliefs, and community (Mays, 2004). One of the main goals for Hull House was to create a forum for people of different backgrounds and experiences to come together in unity to address issues and needs of their community as equals. (Whipps, 2004). Due to the tireless work of Jane Addams, the field of social work has been engaged in the fight for human rights for over 100 years. (Staub-Bernasconi, 2016) The "social work profession can be proud of its heritage as the only help-ing profession imbued with social justice as its fundamental value and concern and a long commitment to peace and human rights" (Lundy & Wormer, 2007, p.728).

Freedom of the mind, body, and spirit was of the utmost importance to Jane in her work with others, especially those who were oppressed and vulnera-ble (Deegan, 2010). It was said that "Addams' nonviolent perspective drew on the work of Gandhi, as well as her family's Quaker religion, to create a feminist and race relations tradition in sociology and the nation." (Deegan, 2010, p.219). One can see many of Addams' values reflected in the International Federation of Social Work's core mandate which states that "a major focus of social work is to advocate for the rights of people at all levels, and to facilitate outcomes where people take responsibility for each other's wellbeing, realize and respect the inter-dependence among people and between people and the environment" (Interna-tional Federation, n.d., Principles para.2).

Peace

Focus on the importance of creating harmony within oneself and within one's com-munity ("Quaker Values", n.d.)

Dignity & Worth of the individual

Treat each person in a caring and respectful fashion, staying mindful of individual differences and cultural/ethnic diversity ("Read the Code," n.d.)

In Addams' day the poor were often viewed through a moralistic lens where fault was assigned due to a weakness of character or corruptibility of the individual. This led to maltreatment and abuse of the poor. Jane embraced a different view based on her Quaker tendencies of believing in the inherent capacity for growth and positivity in everyone (Klosterman & Stratton, 2006). The great depression supported Jane's views that poverty was not a moral flaw but resulted from various environmental factors. She was able to gain support for the implementation of a welfare state from President Roosevelt, who created many programs that assisted with economic security for a multitude of people (Lundblad, 1995). This no doubt helped to bring a modicum of dignity and self-worth back into their lives.

Dieser postulated that Addams Hull House created new understandings and linkages across different cultures through their innovative work blending contact theory with diverse leisure programming (2005). Jane envisioned not a melting pot but a forum of individual citizens from different upbringings/environments with their own voice, point of view, and strengths. She believed this would make our country great (Deegan, 2010). Many immigrants and other oppressed groups never had the opportunity to live a life with dignity on a daily basis. "From their settlement house experiences, they testified...to the massive inequalities of power and wealth and the cultural misunderstandings that continued to divide people" (Sullivan, 1993, p.513). Due to this and their underlying values "they persisted in affirming the possibilities humans have of overcoming their situations through practical actions to transform the word" (Sullivan, 1993, p.514).

One can see how Jane's philosophy influenced the field of social work as they began to seek a unifying mission and shared vision. In their burgeoning code of ethics, they agreed upon the cornerstone value of the "worth and dignity of every human being" (Klosterman & Stratton, 2006 p. 162). This was soon amended to include a "belief that a person's opportunities for growth maximize his or her potential for growth" (Klosterman & Stratton, 2006 p. 162). "Jane...one of the founders of U.S. social work, was an advocate for the full range of human rights. Through both her actions and her writings" (Steen, 2006, p. 101). The NASW is still following in Addams' footprints as seen in the rewriting of their Code of Ethics which included assisting individuals and groups who are vulnerable and oppressed with special attention on respecting difference and diversity, as well as working toward social justice. (Lundy & Wormer, 2007). Due to Jane's influence human rights are reflected and highlighted throughout the cardinal writings that guide social workers both in the United States and internationally (Staub-Bernasconi 2016).

Interestingly the Peace Corp claims a common set of values with both Jane and social work. Jane was applauded for her practice of trusting and empowering the "common man" in exploring ways to find and meet unrecognized social needs. She helped to provide them with a voice and to plan for needed change (Harward, 1963). Harward shared that "She was their great interpreter to the world" (1963, p.15). In 2015 Peace Corp staff found themselves inspired by Jane Addams' Settlement House mission and design. They embarked on a quest to create a Peace Corp Settlement House modeled after many of Hull House's basic tenets. They wanted to "walk their talk" and chose to locate their settlement in a "careworn neglected" neighborhood. Their hope was to impact and empower youth in the neighborhood.

Social work's movement to create local service centers and provide outreach to clients in their communities and homes helps create a deeper understanding for their hardships and daily lives. Jane and the Corp went even further by living side by side with those that they serve (Harward, 1963). There is also a shared call to recognize "our responsibility on an international level. As interrelationships and interdependence of nations increase, responsibility for the welfare of persons in other nations develops accordingly" (Harward, 1963, p.12). This drove much of Jane's international work and has become one of the mandates for the International Federation of Social Workers (IFSW). They state that "Social work seeks to redress historic Western scientific colonialism and hegemony by listening to and learning from Indigenous peoples around the world. In this way social work knowledges will be co-created and informed by Indigenous peoples, and more appropriately practiced not only in local environments but also internationally" (International Federation, n.d., knowledge: para. 2).

Jane was very involved overseas with the peace movement, especially with those whose countries were impacted by the ravages of war (Klosterman & Stratton, 2006). She was appalled by the callousness with which war-torn nations were refused needed aid, and worked tirelessly to overcome those obstacles (Brieland, 1990). Addams was invited to be part of Quaker relief efforts in order to provide for those in need throughout Germany (Klosterman & Stratton, 2006). Jane embraced non-violence as the penultimate way to resolve controversy and obtain social justice, whether between warring nations or divergent cultural values and lifestyles (Deegan, 2010). It has been said that "Jane Addams has been able to do more probably than any other living woman to popularize pacifism and to introduce radicalism into colleges, settlements, and respectable circles." ("Jane Addams", n.d., para. 336).

Jane's platform was that mediation, freedom of personal beliefs, freedom of the press, and community solidarity were all needed to create a healthier and more harmonious world (Sullivan, 1993). The international peacemaking efforts that Jane championed sought an all-encompassing humanitarian process for society whose goal would be to safeguard all life (Klosterman & Stratton, 2006). Today there is a positive move toward preventing global violence through various peaceful means reflected in the Global Fragility Act, which is being considered by the senate at this time (Rowels, 2019). If passed it will provide "efforts around the world, helping places already torn apart by violence to recover and preventing the start of violence in other places where factors are ripe for its outbreak" (Rowels, 2019, para. 3).

Jane made several Quaker connections working with the Women's International League for Peace and Freedom with activists from Swarthmore College. This led to an honorary doctorate degree being granted to her. The college created an archive of her correspondence and works that is still going strong today (Addison & Yoder, 2011). Through her involvement with the Women's International Peace Conference she was able to assist in creating international conditions of peace that still remain an ideal model for peace today (Sullivan, 1993). Jane was recognized for her lifetime of work in this area and was awarded the Nobel Peace Prize for her tireless work towards peace and humanitarianism (Klosterman & Stratton, 2006).

Integrity

Truth and honesty in all of one's dealings ("Quaker Values", n.d.)

Integrity

Act honestly, responsibly, and promote ethical practices ("Read the Code," n.d.)

Hull House utilized "a responsive approach, requiring deep listening to the needs of the community, and identifying solutions with people rather than for them. This approach allowed for a deeper understanding of the issues, and consequently, more lasting solutions" ("Jane Addams and Child Protection", 2016, para. 2). Jane understood the limitations of her own understanding and experiences when it came to serving those in need. She conversed much with her neighbors and all members of her community to start seeking what was truly needed/wanted for positive change. She also utilized community mapping, data gathering, and the lived experiences of her neighbors in studying and planning for change (Deegan, 2016). Addams encouraged Social Workers to be open to learning from others in the community and to embrace their experiences and knowledge (Klosterman & Stratton, 2006).

Hull House was purposely held independent from any organization, religious affiliation, university, or benefactor to support openness and acceptance of all faiths and belief systems for those they served. Jane modeled her beliefs and ideals for inclusiveness and tolerance through her actions, in the underlying philosophy of Hull House and how she treated others. She was passionate about being a steward to those in need, as well as, the community and the world at large (Schultz, 2015). Our current welfare system saw its early beginnings through Jane's good works and political aspirations. Many diverse areas of what became social work were established through her campaigns and contributions ("Jane Addams: Champion," 2016). Addams urged social workers to pursue social reform and embrace advocacy as part of their ethical standards. She believed that by helping to right the hardships of others on the policy and societal level social workers could help improve the lives of many in their communities and beyond (Lundblad,1995).

Jane was concerned with reforming unethical laws and regulations that visited various abuses and trauma on city youth, including poorhouse legislation, criminal proceedings, child labor, and lack of access to schooling towards a more productive future (Long, 1999). Children often had to help supplement family income through various street jobs such as the collecting and selling of junk. The pressure to help support their families could be so great that the children would feel pressured into committing small crimes to help make ends meet (Addams, 1902). The justice system at the time treated both children and adults in the same harsh and retaliatory manner. By today's standards this was a blatant violation of human rights and extremely unethical. She believed that irreparable damage to the youth's future would be caused once they were institutionalized within the adult criminal justice system. The risk for future trauma was very high as was the chance that they might be inducted into a greater life of crime once exposed to the adult criminal element (Zimmering, 2000). For Addams "the first great virtue of the juvenile court was that it would not continue the destructive impact of the criminal justice system on children" (Zimmering, 2000, p.2481). Addams work in child advocacy was a catalyst for the creation of non-punitive juvenile court proceedings outside of the adult legal system, with a focus on treatment rather than sanction (Krisberg, 2006).

The inspiration for the 1st juvenile court grew out of Addams' use of a person in the environment lens. She understood that environmental factors as well as family systems and social challenges needed to be understood in order to establish effective treatment or interventions for youth and to avoid causing more trauma in their already challenging lives (Lacy, 2013). Long described the juvenile system's goal as a "place where specialists could work together to examine a child's character, background, psychology and home environment, and develop a plan of treatment in the child's best interest" (1999, p.2).

Jane lobbied with progressive reformers to pass the Illinois Juvenile Court Act which helped protect children from being tried and punished as adults (Long, 1999). This new paradigm for the juvenile justice system was adopted throughout the United States (Brieland, 1990). The Jane Addams Hull House Association reported that "Jane Addams in the formation of the juvenile justice system, helped reframe cultural and legal interpretations of "the best interests of the child" and prevails today as a foundation for the modern justice system" ("Jane Addams and Child," 2016, para.7). America's current juvenile justice system appears to have swung far from Addams model as there has been an increase in punitive detention centers and trying minors as adults, perhaps we need to revisit and reinvest in her original vision (Krisberg, 2006).

Community

Individuals united for the purpose of a nurturing, dynamic and stable community ("Quaker Values", n.d.)

Importance and centrality of human relationships

Seek to strengthen relationships among people in a purposeful effort to promote, restore, maintain, and enhance well-being for all ("Read the Code," n.d.)

The mission of Hull House was to "provide a center for a higher civic and social life; to institute and maintain educational and philanthropic enterprises; and to investigate and improve conditions in the industrial districts of Chicago" (Addams, 1910, p.112). Addams designed Hull House as a reciprocal learning environment where the staff learned from their neighbors and in turn the community members learned from the staff. It was a cooperative working model where women were seen as equal to men (Lundblad, 1995). Through total immersion in the community Addams was able to see more clearly the manifold variables that affected those in need, as well as the multitude of environmental factors that contributed to many of their challenges. These experiences as well as her research led to community organizing, advocacy, and political action to see to the needs of her neighbors and their families (Klosterman & Stratton, 2006).

Jane's community strengths building involved seeking out and growing local talent. She constantly looked for ways to get neighborhood and city residents involved in leadership roles and service implementation. She trusted in their abilities, vision, and strength (Deegan, 2016). Today the Hull House Association is just as committed to Jane's causes and provides over 100 services to meet a multitude of needs in their community and to improve societal issues. Community members are still an integral part in program planning and provision (Johnson, 1994).

Jane "listened to people's hopes and dreams and saw how they could be implemented" (Deegan, 2016, p.63). Working mothers shared their struggle for a safe haven for children while at work. They also needed support and encouragement from other working moms. Hull House worked with the community to create a day-care and Chicago's first kindergarten. They also provided space and resources for working mothers to meet, create relationships with one another, and share experiences and ideas with each other. This was the beginning of a self-help group process. Jane and Hull House also saw to the expressed lack of recreational/leisure activities for children in the community and helped through organizing the construction of various playgrounds and parks for healthy/safe recreation (Deegan, 2010).

Many older women ended up in dire circumstances with no family ties, social supports, or financial security. Jane as well as other community members took up the call and worked to create supportive relationships and to provide care for these disenfranchised women, many of whom were at risk of being placed, or ended up in the county poor house. She also worked on several commissions and with the community to provide support to both widows and abandoned women. Her work became the springboard for the creation of the Bureau of Organized Charities (Lundblad, 1995).

The rampant spread of urbanization and industrialization of cities created many challenges for the humane treatment and protection of children. As city populations began to boom there were not enough resources for safe housing, decent employment, day care, and access to a regular supply of healthy food (Lacey, 2013). Addams believed that through protecting our children society would benefit in many ways and our country as a whole would have a brighter future. This inspired her to help create the Child Labor Committee to protect children workers from harm. Eventually this movement went national and many social workers and politicians joined their ranks ("Jane Addams and Child Protection," 2016).

Jane spent much of her life seeking protective rights for children as very little precedence existed and constant abuse and advantage was taken of them

("Jane Addams and Child Protection," 2016). She helped to facilitate the inception of the U.S. Children's Bureau and the Federal Child Labor Laws, which set precedence for allowable work hours, age limits, fair wages, and acceptable working conditions for minors ("Jane Addams and Child Protection," n.d.)."

Due to her work to educate the public about the ravages of childhood poverty on the nation as a whole, her efforts were recognized by President Roosevelt who in turn requested her assistance in planning the best way to meet the needs of the nation's dependent children. This brought the profession of Social Work into favor throughout the country (Lundblad, 1995). The field of Social Work often finds itself seeking new solutions to age old challenges such as these. Lundblad shared that in the 90's they faced "deindustrialization of the United States and loss of jobs, inadequate housing, poor health care, the violence of addiction, and discrimination" (1995, P. 668). One can easily see that in 2020 this list is just as relevant as it was in Jane's time and in the 90's. Due to recent technological advances social workers find themselves both with new challenges and helpful resources/tools. They are part of a new globally connected 24-hour world that has created new social connections that are not yet fully understood.

Equality

Respect oneself and others, reject discrimination and injustice, and honor individual differences ("Quaker Values", n.d.)

Social Justice

Seek to promote sensitivity to and knowledge about oppression, cultural and ethnic diversity as well as pursue social change ("Read the Code," n.d.)

Social justice issues were Jane's passion, she worked her entire life on a crusade against abusive and unsafe/unfair working conditions, especially for children. Along with this she supported compulsory education as a means to a healthier future for youth and the nation ("Jane Addams: Champion," 2016). The Hull House Kindergarten became a precursor to compulsory education and created the opportunity for youth to receive early childhood education ("Jane Addams and Child Protection," 2016). Group programming was also provided to serve the many needs of children that public schools were not enabled to meet. They encouraged socialization, imagination and personal initiative (Addams, 1910).

Jane truly believed in and practiced cultural humility/diversity, inclusion, and equality for all (Klosterman & Stratton, 2006). She supported radical change in our nation from governmental ministry to gender, class, and race relations. She conceived that an equal voice for all would lead us to a more balanced age supporting peace and prosperity (Shafer Lundblad, 1995). Citizen schools were created to support equal opportunities and access for all to the full rights of citizenship in the United States. This was not only for immigrants but for women, children, manual workers, the aged, impoverished, and African Americans (Deegan, 2010).

Jane was on a quest to abolish prejudice. "Addams wanted full political citizenship, economic rights and opportunities, and the full interaction of all groups as part of a strong society with multiple meanings and cultures" (Deegan, 2010 p.219). Persecution for political beliefs was seen as a bane to healthy communities and the country. This led to Jane's work in the creation of the American Civil Liberties Union ("Jane Addams," n.d.). Addams also helped form the League for the Protection of Immigrants to address the excessive abuses they so often suffered. She was concerned with segregation of the classes, and where immigrants within these classes were segregated even further. Many families were also caused undue stress due to the younger generations being more assimilated and denying their heritage at times. Many families were adversely affected as a result of these barriers (Lundblad, 1995).

Jane was a purveyor of gender and race equality and through her battle against political corruption helped co-found the National Association for the Advancement of Colored People ("Jane Addams" 2, n.d.). She was also integral to the founding of the National Urban League and was a lifelong member of both organizations. She marched and protested alongside many others to obtain basic human rights, equal access, and social democracy (Deegan, 2010). Through Addams' research and work with the African American community she found that they "faced distinctive difficulties that made their situation even worse than that of the immigrants. In particular, they encountered greater economic and political discrimination, and almost total residential segregation" (Popple, 1996, p113). Jane was appalled by the injustice of the Jim Crow Laws and fought constantly against this form of segregation (Deegan, 2010).

Jane appreciated the Progressive Party's backing for women's emancipation and support of social justice. She wanted the needs of all community members to be heard and ministered to equally (Kitchen, n.d.). Her belief in the strengths and talents of women as well as her work with the National American Woman's Suffrage Association focused on providing equal access to, and opportunities for, economic, social, and political rights (Deegan, 2010). Hull House was instrumental in creating structural change through their work with local and national governing bodies utilizing advocacy for social justice issues and extensive research. This helped pave the way for future social sciences and gave credence to social work as a legitimate profession ("1889 Jane Addams," n.d.) Today's National Association of Social Workers (NASW) has focused on several social justice issues that would have Jane's full backing. These include violations of voting rights, intimate partner abuse, humane immigration policies, effective drug/criminal justice policies, the elimination of racial profiling, and minors being tried/sentenced as adults ("Social Justice," n.d.). One can see many of the social justice issues that Jane worked so tirelessly on reflected in these current challenges.

Stewardship

Analyze the ways in which actions and talents can be used to benefit, rather than harm, each other and the environment ("Quaker Values", n.d.)

Competence

Continually strive to increase knowledge/skills and aspire to contribute to the betterment of the profession ("Read the Code," n.d.)

Deegan stated that "Social equality and cultural pluralism defined Addams and her interactions with her neighbors. Social settlements were full experiments in neighborhood empowerment" (2010, p. 223). Addams embraced the Quaker idiom of "Speaking truth to power," which has become a common social work practice echoing a commitment to assisting those in need through utilizing a strengths perspective and advocating to end injustice and oppression (Klosterman & Stratton, 2006). Addams believed social workers needed to address not only their own community issues but those overseas as well. This was a direct result of the aftermath of World War I and its terrible impact on women, children and families (Klosterman & Stratton, 2006).

Klosterman and Stratton pointed out that "Addams's emphasis on the environment as a basic influence on human behavior and her involvement in social activism to achieve reform marked a fundamental shift in the values base of the emerging social work profession." (2006, p.162). Jane and other staff members of Hull House, as well as local residents, created some of the first sociological research and analysis on many issues they faced in the community. They were able to model services and adjust programming to meet the needs they ascertained (Shafer Lundblad, 1995).

The research that Hull House supported became an actual school for study in the greater scholastic community. They were credited for creating an empirical process for sociological studies and a school that studied racial relations. They used this knowledge to lobby for legislation and services to alleviate the various inequalities they uncovered (Deegan, 2010).

One of the studies they supported delved into the sweatshop trade. Their findings helped pave the way to pass the Illinois Factory Act (Jane Addams, n.d.). Sweatshop labor is still a problematic issue in our economy today. Many US manufacturers utilize them to produce affordable goods with a low overhead. Just as in Jane's time there are still protests against the use of sweatshops and their violations of human rights (Steen, 2006).

Social workers have taken on the mission of protecting and promoting human rights. Steen describes these rights as the entitlement "to freedom...to live without persecution, to express oneself, and to have opportunities to develop (such as through education, health care, and basic economic security)" (2006, p.101). This would require a familiarity with activism, advocacy and various political processes. Many social work practitioners today are focused solely on micro level services and have little involvement at the macro level.

Social workers have been active in the political change process since the 19th century. Involvement in this process has gone in and out of vogue in the field. Those who are involved utilize the scientific problem-solving method to evaluate the effectiveness of their political strategy and its influence on making changes at the policy level (MaHaffey, 1987). As Steen states "Contemporary human rights issues are very similar to those witnessed by Jane Addams... Much like Addams, we live in a time of war" (Steen, 2006, p 102). Due to the 9/11 attack on the United States "Many believe where political rights and civil liberties were once taken for granted, they are now receding" (Steen, 2006, p 102). This can be seen in the US government's adoption of the Patriot Act, which allows violations of citizen civil liberties (Steen, 2006). Today the National Association of Social Workers mandates that social workers challenge social injustice, which would imply that "a knowledge of the political process is therefore essential to achieve change if social work is to live up to the promise of its code of ethics" (MaHaffey, 1987, p.295).

All of Jane's experiences and good works have resulted in quite a legacy. Her deep-seated values have spread far and wide into many other fields and services. Many of her policy and programming creations are still going strong today, while others have morphed into lesser versions of her original design. Through Hull House Jane was able to create a genuine home atmosphere that was welcoming and warm. Modern social service agencies are far from this ideal. They can be cold and clinical with locked doors and shatterproof glass separating clients from those who they seek assistance. This is not the most effective way to connect with others and sends a rather negative message about the clients worth and value (Brieland, 1990). Jane understood connection, community, dignity, and worth. She would certainly encourage a more welcoming and open atmosphere today.

Jane would find a true partner for social justice in 2020 through the Friends Committee on National Legislation (FCNL) as they lobby for many issues that she fiercely advocated for. They mirror her beliefs for what is needed to obtain an inclusive harmonious future for the United States and the world. This can be seen in Randall's statement "The mission for peace, justice, and sustainability is essential for all humanity, regardless of political views" (2019, p.1). FCNL's legislative priorities that both today's social workers and Jane would be passionately involved in include peacebuilding, prevention and diplomacy for armed conflicts; the implementation of an immigration system that provides dignity, respect and basic human rights for all non-citizens; access for all to affordable and fair universal healthcare, and economic justice provided through the support of programs that meet basic human needs ("Our legislative priorities," 2019).

Today's Social Work Grand Challenges have a strong focus on issues that Jane would be all too familiar with, along with some twists unique to the 21st century. They encompass 3 main categories each with several subcategories. Individual and family wellbeing; ensuring healthy development for all youth, closing the health gap, stopping family violence, and advancing long/productive lives: stronger social fabric; eradicating social isolation, ending homelessness, creating social responses to the changing environment, and harnessing technology for social good: a just society; promoting smart decarceration, reducing extreme economic inequality, and achieving equal opportunity and justice (Grand Challenges, n.d.). There are strong Quaker values reflected in these challenges, as seen in some of the parallel work that FCNL is engaged in.

If Jane was a practicing social worker today, she would find herself continuing to advocate for many of the same social justice issues that were of vital importance in the 19th century, perhaps with a slightly different focus. She would embrace the many new challenges in the United States and fully appreciate the international connectedness of today's society. She would be right at home with her principles and values being fully supported through the NASW Code of Ethics, as well as the IFSW's Ethical Principles.

The profession of social work would not look the same or share the same values of service, standing up for human rights and for social justice today if it were not for Jane Addams direct impact on the profession in its infancy. One can see many Quaker values reflected in the core values of social work, their community advocacy and in the work that they engage in. When looking at the Grand Challenges of Social Work there are clear correlations with many of Jane's past goals and social justice work. These grand challenges are also akin to the good works of many Quaker organizations such as FCNL. The social work profession is ever changing but their values always seem to point true north toward the original goals and values created side by side with Jane Addams, her Quaker influences and other amazing social activists and charity workers of her time.

Discussion Questions

1. In what ways have Quaker testimonies/values (SPICES) changed since Jane Addams' day? Is there a different texture to them or any changes in their application, or the communities understanding of them? What connection would Jane feel/have with modern day Quakerism?

2. What cultural, sociopolitical, and economic conditions have influenced changes in social work's core values over time? Would Jane Addams recognize the field today and how would she choose to practice social work?

3. Explore the collaborative possibilities if the Friends Council for National Legislation (FCNL) and the National Association of Social Workers (NASW) combined their visions and resources to work towards social justice, diversity, and inclusion. What would such a collaboration look like, should it be for specific issues or a long-term partnership? What challenges could present themselves through such a collaboration?

4. When looking at current juvenile justice challenges, how have they changed since the inception of the first juvenile justice courts? How does today's proponents of the movement toward more juveniles being tried as adults justify this course of action? Would Jane be up in arms about this practice, if so how might she address it and work towards social change?

5. When reviewing today's social justice issues in comparison to the 1990's as well as in Jane's time are they the same, have they changed, and what progress has been made? What modern tools or connections can be applied to effectively address these social justice issues today?

References

1889 Jane Addams: Settlement work in North America (n.d.). History of social work. Retrieved 5/7/2019 from: https://www.historyofsocial-work.org/eng/details.php?canon_id=137

Addams, J. (1910). *Twenty years at Hull-House.* Phillips Publishing Company.

Addison, B. E. & Yoder, A. M. (2011, January). Jane Addams and the Swarthmore College peace collection. *Peace and Change, 36*(1), 90-96.

Ashley, C. (2019). The power of our witness. *Washington Newsletter Friends Committee on National Legislation,* 789, 4.

Besthorn, F.H. (2002). Expanding spiritual diversity in social work: Perspectives on the greening of spirituality. *Currents: New Scholarship in the Human Services, 1*(1). Retrieved from: https://www.ucalgary.ca/currents/files/currents/v1n1_besthorn.pdf

Brieland, D. (March, 1990). The Hull-House tradition and the contemporary social worker: Was Jane Addams really a social worker? *Social Work, 35*(2), 134-138. https://doi.org/10.1093/sw/35.2.134

Deegan, M. J. (2010). Jane Addams on citizenship in a democracy. *Journal of Classical Sociology, 10*(3), 217-238. DOI: 10.1177/1468795X10371714

Deegan, M.J. (2016). Jane Addams, the Chicago schools of sociology, and the emergence of symbolic interaction, 1889-1935. In Denzin, N. K. (Ed). *The astructural bias change: Myth or reality? Studies in symbolic interaction* (Vol.46), 57-76. Emerald Group Publishing Limited.

Delinquent Children. (1902, May 31). Jane Addams digital edition. Retrieved from: https://digital.janeaddams.ramapo.edu/items/show/1134

Dieser, R. (2005). Understanding how Jane Addams and Hull-House programs bridged cross-cultural differences: Leisure programs and contact theory. *Human Service Education, 25*(1), 53-63.

Grand Challenges. (n.d.). Grand challenges of social work. Retrieved June 19, 2019 from: https://grandchallengesforsocialwork.org/

Harward, N. (1963, October). Peace Corps: The modern Hull House or a to professionalism? *Social Work, 8*(4), pp. 11-17. https://www.jstor.org/stable/23708582

Hebert, T. (2018, July). Toward a peace corps house in Washington, D.C. Retrieved from: https://www.eastoregonian.com/opinion/columnists/toward-a-peace-corps-house-in-washington-d-c/article_616b97d8-8120-5e7c-9da9-354d729f7400.html

International Federation of Social Workers (n.d.) Global definition of social work: Knowledge. Retrieved June 14, 2019 from:

https://www.ifsw.org/what-is-social-work/global-definition-of-social-work/

Jane Addams. (n.d.). Retrieved on June 1, 2019 from: https://spartacus-educational.com/USAaddams.htm

Jane Addams (2). (n.d.). Theodore Roosevelt inaugural. Retrieved on June 14, 2019 from: https://www.nps.gov/thri/jane-addams.htm

Jane Addams: Champion for working poor. (2016). Retrieved from: http://www.digitalhistory.uh.edu/disp_text-book.cfm?smtID=2&psid=3131

Jane Addams and Child Protection. (2016). Jane Addams Hull-House association. Retrieved from: https://janeaddamshullhouse.org/history/jane-addams-and-child-protection/

Johnson, G. (1994, September 16). Jane Addams' spirit of service lives on. *Chicago Tribune.* Retrieved from: https://www.chicagotribune.com/search/dispatcher.front?Query=Jane+Addams%E2%80%99+spirit+of+service+lives+on&target=all&spell=on

Kendall, K. A. (April, 1962). Jane Addams: A product of liberal education. *Social Work, 7*(2)*, 84-88.* https://doi.org/10.1093/sw/7.2.84

Kitchen, A. (nd). Adams, Jane. Retrieved from: https://www.learningtogive.org/resources/addams-jane

Klosterman, E.M. & Stratton, D.C. (2006, May) Speaking truth to power: Jane Addams's values base for peacemaking. *Journal of Women and Social Work, 21*(2), 158-168.

Krisberg, B. (2006) Rediscovering the juvenile justice ideal in the United States. Muncie. J & Goldson, B (Eds.) *Comparative Youth Justice.* Sage.

Lacey, C. (2013, February). Racial disparities and the juvenile justice system: A legacy of trauma. *The National Child Traumatic Stress Network.* Retrieved from: http://www.njjn.org/uploads/digital-library/NCTSN_Racial-disparities-legacy-of-trauma_Clinton-lacey_September%202013.pdf

Long, A. (1999, November). The origins of the juvenile justice system in America. Retrieved from: https://www.wsws.org/en/articles/1999/11/juve-n11.html

Lundy, C. & van Wormer, K. (2007, November 1). Social and economic justice, human rights and peace: The challenge for social work in Canada and the USA. *International Social Work, 50*(6), *727–739.* https://doi.org/10.1177/0020872807081899

Lundblad, K. S. (1995, September). Jane Addams and social reform: A role model for the 1990s. *Social Work, 40*(5), 661. https://doi.org/10.1093/sw/40.5.661

MaHaffey, M. (1987). Political action if social work. In NASW, *Encyclopedia of social work,* (18th ed., Vol 2). National Association of Social Workers.

Mays, D. A. (2004). *Women in early America: Struggle, survival, and freedom in a new world.* ABC-CLIO, Inc.

Molkup, L. V. (1972). Jane Addams by one who knew her, from Jane Addams: A tribute AAUW Chicago branch. Retrieved from: https://aauw-il.aauw.net/files/2013/04/ja_chicago.pdf

Popple, P.R. & Leighninger, L. (1996). *Social work, social welfare, and American society* (3rd Ed). Simon and Schuster Company.

Quaker Values. (n.d.). Retrieved on 6/12/2019 from: https://www.vbf-school.org/quaker-education/quaker-values/

Read the Code of Ethics. (n.d.). NASW. Retrieved on 6/10/2019 from: https://www.socialworkers.org/About/Ethics/Code-of-Ethics/Code-of-Ethics-English

Rowels, B. (May, 2019). The house votes for a new approach to prevent conflict. Friends Committee on National Legislation. Retrieved from: https://www.fcnl.org/updates/the-house-votes-for-a-new-approach-to-prevent-conflict-2084

Ruttum, L. (January, 2011). A librarian's approach to Jane Addams. *Peace and Change, 36*(1). https://doi.org/10.1111/j.1527-2001.2004.tb01292.x

Social Justice Issue Briefs (n.d.). NASW. Retrieved on 6/15/2019 from: https://www.socialworkers.org/Advocacy/Social-Justice/Social-Justice-Issue-Briefs

Staub-Bernasconi, S. (2016, March 21). Social work and human rights: Linking two traditions of human rights in social work. *Journal of Human Rights and Social Work,* 1,40–49. DOI 10.1007/s41134-016-0005-0

Steen, J. A. (April, 2006). The roots of human rights advocacy and a call to action. *Social Work, 51*(2). https://doi.org/10.1093/sw/51.2.101

Sullivan, M. (1993). Social work's legacy of peace: Echoes from the early 20th century. *Social Work, 38*(5), 513-520.

Whipps, J. (2004). Jane Addams's social thought as a model for a pragmatist-feminist communitarianism. *Hypatia, 19*(2), 118-133. https://doi.org/10.1111/j.1527-2001.2004.tb01292.x

Zimring, F. E. (2000). The common thread: Diversion in juvenile justice. *California Literature Review, 88*(6), 247. Retrieved from: https://scholarship.law.berkeley.edu/cgi/viewcontent.cgi?article=1482&context=californialawreview

7 | The Retreat at York: Quaker Mental Health Ministry

By Nelson Bingham

In December, 2018, the institution known as The Retreat in York, England ended its 222-year history of providing in-patient care for those afflicted with mental health problems. This essay is written for the purpose of affirming and, indeed, celebrating that long and distinctive history. We begin by describing The Retreat – what it is and what made it special. How was The Retreat created and how did it evolve over time? What impact has The Retreat had – on the many individuals it has served and on the mental health system?

To understand the power and meaning of The Retreat, it is important that we review the historical context, particularly with regard to the way in which the behaviors that we now consider "mental illness" were viewed and handled by society. Terms such as "madness," "lunacy," or "insanity" were commonly applied to individuals whose behaviors fell outside the boundaries of "normalcy." Such conditions, many found across all cultures, are today diagnosed into categories such as schizophrenia, autistic spectrum disorders, bi-polar disorders, paranoia, etc. In England, one of the most famous instances of madness was the situation of King George III. Glover (1984) described the way in which he developed an illness now known as porphyria in 1788. His symptoms included extreme agitation, talkativeness, hoarseness, colic, insomnia, lack of appetite, fever, and most dramatically, extreme mental confusion. The latter, especially in light of the inability of court physicians to diagnose his physical problem, led to a widespread public attribution of "madness." The King was subjected to many of the common (and generally distasteful) treatments with no success. His general popularity led to wide public attention to the phenomenon of madness and to some increase in sympathy for the insane. But it did not result in any significant change in treatment.

The prevailing cultural paradigm of Europe in the eighteenth century viewed human beings as created (in the Judeo-Christian tradition) God's image, most particularly as endowed with the capacity for rational thinking. As noted by Borthwick et. al (2001), this was rooted in "the Cartesian ideal that Reason and Logic formed the basis of all nature and that this was glorified and exemplified in the human being, God's supreme creation" (p. 428). Therefore, any individual human being who lacked (or came to lack) such rationality could not be considered to have the status of a person. The implication of this was that such an individual was reduced to, and accorded no more rights and compassion than, a lower animal.

There were vigorous debates regarding the causes of such "insanity" (Stewart, 1992), ranging from demonic possession to hereditary defects to iatrogenic factors (e.g. improper uses of mercury in medical treatment) to medical disorders to environmental stresses. Ideas about causation, naturally, gave rise to theories of treatment. Those who believed in spiritual origins tended toward religious approaches (e.g. exorcism). Those who were inclined to medical explanations often employed rather extreme physical remedies (e.g. bleeding, emetics, purges, immersion into hot or cold baths, poultices on the feet). Those whose explanation for madness favored inheritance were generally pessimistic about any such cures. In such instances, chronic confinement was seen as the only option. Even those who received the various aforementioned treatments generally required ongoing confinement. There are anecdotal reports of some recoveries, but the lack of good records generally prevents drawing any solid conclusions.

In many cases, those deemed insane were left in the care of families (often restrained or confined at home) or condemned to roam about until they created enough trouble as to be imprisoned. Glover (1984) describes the creation of a number of "asylums" in England, starting with Bethlem in London. Founded in 1247, that institution officially became an asylum for the insane in 1377. Over the next several centuries, a variety of private and public "madhouses" arose with most providing very limited care for their residents. One of these was the York Lunatic Hospital, founded in 1777.

By 1774, as noted by Glover (1984), some effort at providing legal protections was made but the system so created struggled with three challenges – protecting the public from the threat (some real and much imagined) of lunatics, protecting innocent citizens from unjust confinement in asylums, and insuring ethical treatment of those who truly required confinement.

The lack of any consensus regarding appropriate treatment meant that most persons deemed insane were subjected to inhumane confinement. Many were chained and/or kept locked in isolation. While, in some ways, this was understandable, given the unpredictability of their behaviors, it undoubtedly also contributed to an exacerbation of their symptoms, resulting in a vicious cycle. Glover (1984) analyzes such treatment in terms of the prevailing belief in human rationality as the hallmark of personhood. Lacking that capability, it was all-too-tempting to see the insane as sub-human animals without typical human feelings and morality and without the ability to ever learn to participate in human society. The common assumption was that, in the absence of Reason, only Fear could exert necessary control over the behaviors of captive "creatures." Glover (1984) notes that, "the first principle in handling the insane was to instill fear" (p. 4). Unfortunately, as Glover (1984) also acknowledges, "Fear and anger are close akin and both may release adrenalin into the blood stream, so that the creature, man or beast, becomes more ferocious and more dangerous" (p. 5). The widespread use of restraints very likely led to a condition studied by modern psychologists known as "learned helplessness," characterized by further withdrawal and alienation from possible human engagement. As Glover points out, there is a reciprocal effect on those who care for the insane in such a situation – "men's hearts on this subject become gradually hardened" (p. 7) (a process known by psychologists today as "cognitive dissonance").

Such was the context in which William Tuke sought to establish The Retreat in York in 1792. Tuke's motives for doing so arose, in no small part, from his Quaker identity. The Quaker movement, begun by George Fox in 1652, had developed over the following 140 years into a sect with highly distinctive characteristics. As Borthwick et al. (2001) note, Quakers emphasized "the individual's responsibility to cultivate a lifestyle which would encourage and nurture the 'Inner Light'" which led to "Quaker insistence on the spiritual equality of all human beings" (p. 428). This was often described in terms of "That of God in Every Person." This core Quaker belief in human equality before God led directly to the spiritual and moral imperative to "…be committed to the effort to make contact with that of God in everyone" (Glover, 1984, p.14). This had, of course, been the basis of the longstanding Quaker effort to improve the condition of those who were imprisoned. Indeed, as Glover describes, during "…the late 18th century…a new concern for social welfare was growing in the Society [of Friends]" (p. 14). Borthwick et al. (2001) speculated that more than 150 years of "relentless persecution suffered by the early Quakers led them to form a system of mutual solidarity" (p. 428) such that, even when such persecution diminished (by the late eighteenth century), there remained a kind of "collective consciousness" among Friends that manifested itself as "empathy with marginalized members of society."

It was within this framework that William Tuke became aware in 1792 of the case of Hannah Mills. Glover (1984) reports that Mills, a Quaker widow who had begun showing signs of insanity in 1790, was confined in the York Asylum. It was the practice of Quaker meetings at that time to send a group of members to visit a person who was so confined, but such a group was denied permission to visit Hannah Mills whose physical condition deteriorated until she died a few months later. Apparently, based on what rumors were available, York Friends came to suspect that conditions in the York institution were inhumane and, indeed, shocking. Tuke's daughter, Ann, discussed this with her family and suggested that Friends should create a place where their members suffering from insanity could receive proper care. Her father, William, felt a strong leading from God to pursue such a goal. After some debate within the York Quarterly Meeting, he did act to establish The Retreat. There is no direct evidence that Tuke was specifically influenced by Biblical injunctions, but we might imagine that his leading could be consistent with Matthew 25:40, which states, "The King will reply, 'Truly I tell you, whatever you did for one of the least of these brothers and sisters of mine, you did for me."

From the beginning, Tuke and his son, Henry (and, later his grandson, Samuel) strived to create in The Retreat an environment that embodied Quaker beliefs and principles. This would be an environment that stood in stark contrast to the then-prevailing approaches to dealing with lunacy or madness. This required several important steps – building an appropriate physical facility, acquiring a staff to enact the distinctive philosophy and treatment, creating supportive programs and practices, and most basically, gaining sufficient support from Friends to fund this enterprise. Not surprisingly, the process took some time. With planning begun in 1792, it was not until 1796 that The Retreat was ready to receive its first patients.

Tuke himself was financially comfortable but hardly wealthy enough to provide the funds for The Retreat. Much of his energy, therefore, had to go into persuading others (including individuals and Meetings) to "subscribe" by providing set amounts (with the associated privilege of allowing a family member or Meeting member, as needed, to receive care at The Retreat). Eventually, financial considerations led to allowing non-Friends with the means to pay to receive such care.

So, what was this special care that was offered? There have been a number of helpful accounts written on this subject. Probably, the most well-known and useful was *The Description of The Retreat* by Tuke (1813), William's grandson who was directly involved in the development and management of the institution in its earliest days. In that text, Reverend Sydney Smith, notes, "The great principle on which it appears to be conducted is that of kindness to the patients" (p. 5). In the Introduction to that book, Hunter and Macalpine state, "The prospect of freeing the insane from neglect, maltreatment, chains and starvation found more ready echo in the hearts of social reformers and humanitarians than in the narrower views and vested interests of medical and non-medical madhouse keepers" (p. 5). Samuel Tuke (1813) described the aim of The Retreat as striving to provide a "milder and more appropriate system of treatment" (p. 22) for those members of the Society of Friends who were "laboring under that most afflictive dispensation – the loss of reason" (p. 24).

In the construction of the facilities of The Retreat, emphasis was placed on providing for the "cure and comfort" of the patients, "… as much considered as security." Distinctive features of the facility included, according to Glover (1984), "long wide corridors…to enable restless patients to walk up and down, windows to allow for ample light (avoiding the appearance of a prison), outside gardens wherein patients could undertake meaningful work" (p. 31). An interesting example of the humane treatment of patients was the fact that among the first purchases by William Tuke were beds and spoons (it was customary in madhouses of the time for patients to sleep on straw and to eat food, when it was provided at all, with bare hands).

Even more important than the physical setting was the social environment that was created at The Retreat. Glover (1984) indicates that, "The problem of finding staff was not easy…Tuke wanted men and women who were Quakers, and were kind and reliable" (p. 35). Glover describes a number of early staff who embody the spirit desired. These include: Timothy Maud, Thomas Fowler, Ann Retton, Katherine Allen and George Jepson. Among these individuals, Thomas Fowler, a medical doctor, stands out. He was a dedicated scientist who rigorously studied the effects of the best medical wisdom of the time for the treatment of the insane. That included bleeding, blistering, emetics and more, but Fowler, finding no consistent improvements due to such treatments, finally abandoned all of them, clearing the way for the staff of The Retreat to employ what would become its signature approach – moral treatment. This being said, Glover (1984) concludes that, "The main reason why The Retreat survived the precarious early years was that William Tuke had exactly the qualities needed by a man responsible for such a project. The Retreat was a challenge to him…His compassion, combined with his buoyancy and indefatigable energy and his gift for leadership, made him the ideal person for this demanding assignment" (p. 52).

According to Glover (1984), Tuke was adamant about two characteristics necessary for treatment of the insane – "The first was that they need as much physical comfort as possible…they should be clothed, as many lunatics were not; fed, although many lunatics were starved to reduce their strength; clean; and treated with kind civility…William Tuke's second preconceived idea about the management of the insane was that they should be kept 'quiet and still'" (p. 38-39). This second idea was "thought to be quite impractical. Most asylums seem to have been full of noise, if not turbulence, most of the time" (p. 39). It is likely that the lack of chains and the very limited use of confinement at The Retreat, coupled with Tuke's (and, later, Jepson's) calm and patient approach to any incipient disturbance contributed to the notable atmosphere of quiet in The Retreat.

As Superintendent of The Retreat, George Jepson came up with a key insight that would form the basis of the approach of moral treatment. Glover (1984) reports that,

> The daily management of patients was carried out with gentleness…some had meals at common tables, some in their rooms, to be supervised to prevent altercations developing into fighting; some of them would have to see the doctor, some to be set to work on various occupations. In all of this, he observed their reactions to kindness and soon changed his ideas about the condition of their minds; he saw that they were not like wild beasts, nor bereft of reason. They were human beings in whom reason had been impaired, but not destroyed. He found that by appealing to their reasonableness and affection and their desire to be respected, he could give them confidence and gain their co-operation (p. 56).

In his Description of The Retreat (1813), Samuel Tuke (1813) provided an extensive account of the approach of moral treatment. He begins by noting that The Retreat "fully unites with the intelligent Dr. Pinel, in his comparative estimate of moral and medical science" (Tuke, 1813 p. 132) Pinel, of course, is well-known for his own humane treatment of the insane in France. A key assumption of moral treatment is that, "Insane persons generally possess a degree of control over their wayward propensities. Their intellectual, active, and moral powers, are usually rather perverted than obliterated" (Tuke, 1813, p. 133). Further, Tuke explains that the emotional estrangement is most frequently a result (rather than a cause) of the ways in which well-meaning family, friends, and/or professionals have attempted to manage their behaviors. In contrast, the approach of moral treatment is built upon the aim of encouraging self-regulation by the insane person, something that is more realistic if the induction of fear in the patient can be avoided.

Tuke (1813) notes, considering the key features of moral treatment, that, "...they regard the comfort of insane persons; but they are of far greater importance, as they relate to the cure of the disorder. The patient feeling himself of some consequence, is induced to support it by the exertion of his reason, and by restraining those dispositions, which, if indulged, would lessen the respectful treatment he receives or lower his character in the eyes of his companions and attendants" (p. 159) He adds,

> considerable advantage may certainly be derived, in this part of moral management, from an acquaintance with the previous habit, manners, and prejudices of the individual. Nor must we forget to call to our aid, in endeavouring to promote self-restraint, the mild but powerful influence of the precepts of our holy religion. Where these have been strongly imbued in early life, they become little less than principles of our nature; and restraining power is frequently felt, even under the delicious excitement of insanity (p 160-161).

In utilizing moral treatment, Tuke (1813) advises that self-restraint may be promoted by attendants who,

> ought sedulously to endeavor to gain their confidence and esteem; to arrest their attention, and to fix it on objects opposite to their illusion; to call into action, as much as possible, every remaining power and principle of the mind; and to remember that, in the wreck of the intellect, the affections not infrequently survive (p. 162).

It is not generally advisable for attendants or others to argue against a patient's hallucinations or distorted beliefs, which tends to provoke emotions of anger and/or fear. Hence, distraction and calm acceptance are likely to work better than coercion. For behaviors such as refusal to eat, patience and persuasion are preferred to attempts at compulsion. Of course, there are some few cases where a patient's behaviors represent an immediate danger to self or others. As a last resort, Tuke (1813) indicates that coercive techniques may be employed, but this should still be done with care for the comfort and dignity of the patient.

Moral treatment of the insane was, thus, a hallmark of The Retreat from its inception. This approach was a natural expression of the Quaker faith of the Tuke family and of others who gave early support to this enterprise. Treating patients, first and foremost, as persons in whom the Light of God was inherent, was at the heart of their holistic approach, characterized by gentleness, humanity and respect. This meant rejecting most of the common practices found in insane asylums of the eighteenth century, including chaining, isolated confinement, abusive coercion, starving, cold baths, bleeding, emetics, and more. In a more positive vein, the use of moral treatment included treating the patient as a partner who must be supported in self-regulation, providing an environment that allows freedom of movement, clean beds, natural light, supplying good food (and even drink!), involving the patient in meaningful work, and enabling them to interact with staff and other patients. Indeed, regular opportunities for worship were a part of life in The Retreat.

More recently, Borthwick et al. (2001) reported that, "many of the core principles which guided the pioneers of The Retreat 200 years ago are still relevant to contemporary mental health issues" (p. 427). Those authors identify seven core principles of moral treatment. Those are (p. 431):

- A concern for the human rights of people with severe and disabling mental health problems
- Personal respect for people with severe mental health problems
- An emphasis on the healing power of everyday relationships
- The importance of useful occupation
- Emphasis on the social and physical environment
- A common-sense approach rather than reliance on technology or ideology
- A spiritual perspective

What were the effects or outcomes of this model of mental health treatment? There are at least three kinds of answers to this question. First, how effective was moral treatment in helping the insane individuals to improve? Second, what impact did the philosophy and practice of The Retreat have upon the broad system of treatment of mental health problems? Third, how did The Retreat exemplify and contribute to the ministry of the Society of Friends?

With respect to individual outcomes, the staff at The Retreat kept comprehensive written records for patients, including personal history, symptoms, treatments, and outcomes. Borthwick (2001, personal communication) shared historical patient records that showed a sample of individuals of widely varying ages admitted in 1809 and discharged as improved within a year or two (personal communitacation). Glover (1984) reports that Samuel Tuke, in his *Description of The Retreat* (1813) "gives some careful statistics…from 1796-1811, 149 patients had been admitted, sixty of whom had only recently become ill, and eighty-nine who had been ill for some time. Of the sixty recent cases, forty recovered and eight improved" (p. 69).

It is difficult to demonstrate conclusively how The Retreat compared with other asylums of the eighteenth and nineteenth century because of the lack of comparable records. Nonetheless, it is clear that the approach of moral treatment represented a growing spirit of humanistic approaches to mental health. A major factor in this movement was the publication of Samuel Tuke's *Description of The Retreat* in 1813. The cover to that book states,

> In 1796, William Tuke and his fellow Quakers opened The Retreat and embarked on a revolution in the humane treatment of people suffering from mental illness...became one of the founding documents of modern psychiatry. Personal relationships and social expectations were seen as the keys to therapeutic change...Yet by the end of the 19th century moral treatment had all but vanished, debased by the sheer size of the county asylums and overshadowed by biological and individualistic approaches to treatment...In the final decades of the 20th century it seems that the pendulum has once more swung towards an individualistic approach to mental illness. We need now to ask how the social values that gave rise to moral treatment can again be [used] to steer us towards a new response to the presence of mental illness in our society (Tuke, 1813, back cover page).

The publication of Samuel Tuke's *Description of The Retreat*, Glover (1984) reports, led to positive reviews, such as one by Reverend Sydney Smith, which gave it "unqualified and astonished approval" (Glover, 1984, p. 51). This, in turn, gave rise to "streams of visitors" from both within England and abroad, including a number of Russians of nobility. Glover (1984) notes that, "all of this was very valuable publicity for The Retreat" (p. 73). She notes, further, that "Dr. Duncan of Edinburgh, said that "The Retreat has demonstrated beyond contradiction the very great advantage resulting from a mode of treatment ... much more mild than was before introduced to almost any asylum" (Glover, 1984, p. 73). A public conflict arising around the quality of care provided by the York Asylum, following publication of Tuke's book, not only created public attention that led to improvements in that institution, but more broadly, to national political events culminating in 1828 with a law that set up public asylums, many of which were "largely modeled on The Retreat, both with regard to building design and also principles of management." (Glover, 1984, p. 76).

One notable example of the wider impact of The Retreat is the Friends Hospital in Philadelphia Pennsylvania, the history of which was described in a New York Times article on April 17, 1988. This first private psychiatric hospital in the United States was founded in 1813 as the Friends Asylum for the Relief of

Persons Deprived of the Use of Reason. According to that article, "Thomas Scattergood, a Philadelphia tanner who suffered bouts of depression, visited The Retreat at York, a Quaker hospital for the insane. Mr. Scattergood was so impressed by the kind of care that he saw in England that, as he later wrote, he 'vented a few tears.' Mr. Scattergood brought the concept of moral treatment back to Philadelphia and became one of the founders of the Friends Hospital." Friends Hospital, like its "parent," The Retreat, still operates by Quaker principles and practices, notably utilizing moral treatment.

While The Retreat was, thus, an important influence upon the movement toward more humane care of the insane, it must be acknowledged that no such movement occurs in a vacuum. As Glover (1984) explains,

> the principle of non-restraint … did not become universal. There would seem to have been several reasons for this…the hospitals that did adopt the principle were not always completely successful…The medical profession were slow to be convinced that non-violence was really the best method for dealing with insanity…there were other considerations…A very powerful one was the obsession with money [and its corollary, efficiency]. It costs more to run an asylum without physical restraint … you have to have enough attendants" (p. 78).

Glover (1984) further notes that, in England, the mental health activist, Lord Shaftesbury, eventually accepted "his awareness that the House of Commons had tired of his appeals to their compassion and of his efforts to get legislation to mitigate the wretchedness of helpless people who could not help themselves; [including] the insane" (p. 79).

It is beyond the scope of this essay to trace in any detail the broader history of the treatment of those afflicted with mental health problems. Through the 19th and 20th centuries, such treatment evolved in a variety of ways. A plethora of psychological therapies came onto the scene. A number of more modern medical techniques came into being (e.g. lobotomies, electroshock therapy). Pharmacological products replaced chains as a means of controlling aberrant behaviors (and thoughts and feelings). Some of these approaches allowed for extensive de-institutionalization as many patients were sufficiently managed that they could live independently. Throughout this time, philosophical debates continued regarding the status of patients. To what extent can they truly live autonomous lives, characterized by free will and rationality? To what extent do drugs promote a mechanistic image of persons that, indeed, de-humanizes them?

In a more positive vein, however, the quest for a more humanistic approach continues. In fact, it is alive and well in places such as The Retreat[1] and Friends Hospital. In such settings, Friends were not single-mindedly focused, from the start, on the effectiveness of moral treatment in curing insanity. As noted by Glover (1984), "What they had set their hearts on was not cure, a word they would never use; but that deranged Quakers might have their illness in peace and comfort, and if possible, improve in general health" (p. 48). In short, the most basic motive that shaped the creation of The Retreat was the unwavering conviction that every person has the Light of God within. In this regard, the motive was the same as that which led Quakers to concerns about those who were imprisoned, to oppose slavery (eventually), to pacifism and non-violence, and to work for justice. William Tuke may have hoped that the insane who were recipients of moral treatment would regain their full mental faculties, but in the meantime (or even if that improvement never happened), they deserved humane, compassionate care. Tuke was committed to this because it was the right thing to do!

In fact, the use of moral treatment of the insane at The Retreat (and elsewhere) was not only the right thing to do for those patients. Equally, it was necessary in order to answer That of God in the caregivers as well, to sustain their humanity. The Retreat and its distinctive approach of moral treatment should be seen as an expression of Quaker ministry.

Discussion Questions

1. How is the approach of "moral treatment" of mental illness an expression of Quaker beliefs and ideals?

2. William Tuke had a leading to create The Retreat. What did he hope to accomplish with this new institution?

3. What were the effects or outcomes of The Retreat and its new model of mental health treatment? How lasting have those effects been?

---

[1] On December 31, 2018, The Retreat ended its 222-year history of inpatient treatment. It will continue to handle outpatient services including those for autism and ADHD. This will not change the fundamental spirit of moral treatment for those served by The Retreat.

References

Borthwick, A., Holman, C., Kennard, D., McFetridge, K. M. & Wilkes, J. (2001). The relevance of moral treatment to contemporary mental health care, *Journal of Mental Health*, 10 (4), 427-439.

Glover, M. (1984), *The Retreat at York: An early experiment in the treatment of mental illness*. William Sessions Limited.

Stewart, K. A. (1992). *The York Retreat: in the light of the Quaker Way*. William Sessions Limited.

Tuke, S. (1813). *Description of The Retreat, an institution near York for insane persons of the Society of Friends*. Process Press.

8 | Quaker Relations with Midwestern Native Americans

By Max L. Carter

In the recent revision of Quaker history that has included a more critical look at Friends' attitudes about race and women's rights, Friends' record on relations with Native Americans has also come under criticism. Clyde Milner II's *With Good Intentions* (University of Nebraska Press, 1982) and the October 2016 issue of *Friends Journal* are but two examples of writing that has burst the bubble of "Quaker exceptionalism" when it comes to European Christian engagement with Indians. Much earlier, though, Robert Berkhofer, Jr.'s *Salvation and the Savage* (1965) noted that while most Christian groups' encounter with Indians was motivated by an intent to convert them in order that they might then become "civilized," Quakers sought first to "civilize" them in order that they might then become Christian.

Institutional and individual Quaker work with Native Americans in the Midwest in the early 1800s both confirms and offers exceptions to Quaker "exceptionalism." By the standards of the day, Quaker establishment of an agricultural mission among Native American tribes in northeastern Indiana in 1804 was progressive. Friends were responding to an invitation from the Indians themselves; they did not build a boarding school or try to change Indian culture; they did not view the Indians as "savages." It is instructive to recall that the first whites to be convicted in Indiana for murdering Indians didn't occur until 1824. Yet there were still examples in the Quaker work of attitudes that wouldn't pass the "smell" test by the standards of today.

The Work Begins

Programmatic Quaker relations with Indians in the Midwest resulted from a visit among Friends in Baltimore by Miami chief Little Turtle (Mihsihkinaahkwa) and Potawatomi chief Five Medals (Wannangsea). Returning from a trip to memorialize Congress in opposition to the liquor trade, the two chiefs met with the Indian Committee of Baltimore Yearly Meeting in late December of 1801 and requested assistance in turning to settled agriculture following the loss of their hunting lands. As a result, the Meeting for Sufferings of Baltimore Yearly Meeting approved up to $400 for the purchase of agricultural equipment to be sent to Fort Wayne, Indiana, for Little Turtle to distribute (Minutes, n.d.).

Subsequently, a large shipment of implements was sent, but a letter from Little Turtle and Five Medals in 1803 indicated that the people were not as inclined toward learning how to cultivate the land as the two chiefs had hoped. They asked Friends in Baltimore to visit them for the purpose of ascertaining whether they could offer further assistance. Accordingly, in early 1804 a delegation of Friends undertook the journey.

While it appears that Friends were acting in response to the request of the Indian chiefs, there is circumstantial evidence that government policy may have influenced them as well. In 1802, Congress passed a law providing the president with the power to furnish Indians with agricultural equipment and advisors to encourage farming rather than hunting. $15,000 was appropriated for the initiative. The particulars of the legislation were included in the minutes of Baltimore Yearly Meeting in 1802. It is clear from later minutes, however, that the Friends who traveled to Indiana in 1804 were not government agents.

Meeting in Fort Wayne with a large assembly of Indians summoned by Little Turtle and Five Medals, the delegation sought to assure their "red brethren" (as they referred to them in reports shared in Baltimore) that their only motivation was love and a concern that they needed to change their mode of living if they were to survive, explaining that they could help maximize the benefits of the tools already sent. To further emphasize the point, the Friends told of how their European ancestors had "lived as the Indians did" before prospering with changes introduced by "people from the East." Furthermore, one of the members, Philip Dennis, would remain with the Indians to give instructions in farming with no recompense from the Indians.

The contents of the Friends' speech make it clear that they had no intention of evangelizing the Indians. No mention of religion was made, except for expressions of thanks to the Great Spirit for giving the Indians lands that were ideal for raising crops and herds of cattle. They had no such reservations, however, about emphasizing that the Indians would have to change certain aspects of their culture. Specifically, the Indians were told that the men would need to start working in the fields rather than women. "Women are less than men," the Quakers told the assembly; "they are not as able to endure fatigue as men" (Minutes, 1804).

Little Turtle responded to the Friends' words positively and said that their young men needed to adopt the plan in all its particulars, noting that he and Five Medals had already agreed on a site for an agricultural mission near their respective villages. The delegation was then taken to the site, 33 miles southwest of Fort Wayne on the Wabash River. After a frosty April night of fitful sleep with noises of otters splashing, deer whistling, wolves howling, and turkeys gobbling, the Friends staked out the fields to be cleared and began constructing a temporary shelter for Dennis.

Dennis remained through the growing and harvesting seasons, expressing some loneliness, but registering no regrets, given the distressed situation of the Indians themselves. Returning to Maryland in the fall, he reported that the venture had been a modest success. Only one Indian family had settled at the mission, but other Indians worked industriously with him. Their efforts resulted in 400 bushels of corn and a bounty of turnips, potatoes, cucumbers, watermelons, pumpkins, beans, parsnips, and other vegetables. There were 23 hogs raised, seven of which, totaling 1,500 lbs., were ready for slaughter. Dennis also mentioned that the women had wanted to help in the fields, but he had discouraged them, introducing them instead to spinning and knitting with the aid of spinning wheels that had been sent for that purpose. The chiefs remained supportive of the efforts but continued to urge caution in expecting too rapid a change in the Indians' lifestyle (Minutes, 1805).

The work continued to expand in subsequent years, with additional workers sent from Baltimore and increasing numbers of Indians visiting what became known as "Dennis's Station." Another delegation from Baltimore Yearly Meeting visited in the spring of 1808 to consult with the Indians about the work. Assurances were given to the Indians that if they wanted Quaker workers to continue to instruct them, they would. Otherwise, they would leave. One of the chiefs, White Loon (Wapamangwa), expressed appreciation for the good relations that had existed between Indians and Quakers since the time of Onas (William Penn) and proceeded to contrast the actions of other white settlers with those of Friends. He maintained that the Indians recognized the need to turn to agriculture and trusted the Quakers to give them the needed assistance.

Work in Indiana Ends

Unfortunately, work at Dennis's Station was suspended in 1810 among increasing tensions preceding the War of 1812. The following year, the decisive Battle of Tippecanoe was fought near Lafayette, Indiana, resulting in the defeat of Indian forces led by Tecumseh. A terse statement entered in the minutes of Baltimore Yearly Meeting in 1812 noted that Dennis's Station had been destroyed by Indians friendly to Great Britain.

In a report prepared by Baltimore Yearly Meeting reflecting on the work in Indiana, the Indian Committee said that, while the project had not been as successful as they had hoped, some Indians had benefited from it and that the primary object of the work had been to introduce the arts of civil life to the Indians. These goals, as reported, were seen as necessary preliminaries to religious improvement and education, but no schools had been attempted (Minutes, 1812).

The demise of Dennis's Station did not mean the end of Baltimore Friends' work among the Indians of the Midwest. It was moved to Ohio, where the same pattern of agricultural instruction and cultural alteration was continued. Similar to the Wabash mission, the program in Ohio was basically free of any attempt at proselytizing, although the introduction of "civilization" was seen as preliminary to religious improvement.

Work in Ohio

Moving the work to Wapakoneta among the Shawnee was facilitated by Indian agent John Johnston, who was familiar with Friends through his marriage to a Quaker and was supported by the revered Shawnee chief Black Hoof (Catecahassa). Upon hearing from Johnston that Quakers were willing to move their operation to Ohio, the elderly chief responded, "What you said concerning the Quakers we believe is entirely true, and we want them to come on and assist us as soon as possible" (Hill, 1957 p. 51).

In 1811, work commenced on building saw and grist mills at Wapakoneta, and agricultural tools were sent to another Indian village nearby. A family was not found to operate the grist mill when it was completed in 1812, however, as the outbreak of war embroiled the region. By the time peace was restored in 1815, the grist mill had been destroyed. Funds from the Baltimore Indian Committee and assistance from the newly formed Ohio Yearly Meeting Indian Committee insured that the mill was rebuilt in 1816, and Ohio Friends appointed a family to take charge of the mill. Reports back to the two committees said that Indians had helped with the repairs to the mill and that they were uniformly sober, industrious, cheerful, and willing to be instructed.

Work in Wapakoneta among the Shawnee was affected, however, by continued anxiety among the Indians that the U.S. government had intentions of moving them beyond the Mississippi. Treaties continued to extinguish their claims to land, and by 1818 the 559 Shawnee at Wapakoneta were reduced to a ten square mile reservation. And that land, they heard, was being threatened by white settlers who were conspiring to break up the Quaker establishment and induce the Indians to leave. In response, Friends sent a letter to President Monroe arguing against Indian removal and giving examples of the successes of the Quaker work in introducing the "necessary arts of civil life" and "preparing their minds for the reception of the light of the Gospel" (Minutes of Ohio Yearly Meeting, 1818, October 11).

Growing unease over the threat of Indian removal was not the only tension felt. In 1819 Congress passed the Indian Civilization Act, making funds available for establishing schools and other projects. Some Friends saw it as an opportunity to expand the work in Ohio, while others were hesitant about becoming agents of the government and being forced to conform to policies inconsistent with Quaker principles. Another concern was that unless the threat of white encroachment on Indian lands was to be addressed, work among the Indians had little long term prospect of success. Ultimately, the decision was made not to accept federal funds, but Ohio's Indian Committee expressed its disagreement with Baltimore over the decision.

Isaac Harvey, a Friend from Southwestern Ohio, became the superintendent of the work at Wapakoneta in 1819 and immediately faced a challenge that some of the Shawnee leaders were encouraging a move with other tribes to western lands, leading to some unrest and neglect of field work. The disturbance soon passed, however, and herds, crops, and gardens were soon in good order - - and a new saw mill produced 12,000 feet of planks in its first year.

Harvey was soon confronted with another problem, however. The Prophet (Tenskwatawa), a Shawnee religious leader and younger brother of Tecumseh, was in the community applying traditional methods of addressing what was believed to be spells of witchcraft. It became quite personal when a woman accused of witchcraft and threatened with execution sought refuge in the superintendent's home. Threatening to leave the community if the Indians did not abandon the idea of killing the woman, Harvey met with a council of Shawnee chiefs to discuss the matter, the end result being that the Indians expressed their desire for the Quakers to stay and guaranteed the safety of the woman, but also abandoned the practice of witchcraft.

The Focus of Work Shifts

While the mills continued successful operation and field work produced good crops, the ongoing anomie of a culture in erosion through the loss of traditional ways of life, the constant threat of removal, and the effects of alcohol led Friends to propose two actions: the establishment of a school and a move of the center of Quaker work to a farm outside the Shawnee reservation -- so as not to give the appearance of taking over Indian properties. By boarding children at a Quaker school, it was argued, "habits not yet fully developed could be reformed and the young people directed to the proper social, civil, and religious duties" (Minutes, 1821).

According to plan, 214 acres of land were purchased across the reservation line, and a cabin was built for the superintendent and one for a school. Indians assumed the operation of the mills in Wapakoneta. The school opened in 1822 with Chief Black Hoof in attendance. Telling Friends that he believed their intentions were good and that the children had no prospect of living the life their ancestors had formerly lived, he encouraged the Quaker educational project to deal tenderly and respectfully with the children.

Black Hoof continued by asking Friends to consider the spiritual welfare of the students as well. But he urged respect for the Shawnees' own modes of worship, commenting that Quaker and Shawnee spiritual practices were similar. "Like us, when you meet together on occasions for devotion, you speak to the people without so much singing and praying" (Harvey, 1855, p. 180). On another occasion, the ancient chief had noted that Friends, like the Shawnee, waited in silence for the Spirit to sing among them.

Friends heeded the chief's advice and did not require the Indian children to attend Quaker worship. Worship did occur, but it was held in the privacy of the superintendent's own home. During the first year of operation, the school enrolled 12 students, the subject matter including vocational skills along with reading and writing. Subsequent years, however, saw only sporadic attendance at the school, with frequent turnover of superintendents and teachers leading to suspension of the school for long stretches of time. And then in 1825 the first significant removal of the Shawnee to Missouri occurred. With the government encouraging removal and the desire of white settlers for the Indians' lands, prospects for the school and farm were dim, but the Wapakoneta Shawnee decided to remain.

By 1826, other concerns were emerging. A revival of traditional Indian spiritual practices was taking place, and that was leading to a lessening of the Shawnees' support for the school. There was also a growing concern among the Indians about the Quakers' own fidelity to their religious traditions. Chief Black

Hoof stated it directly: "When I first met the Quakers, they could be distinguished from others by simple dress which had been a preservation in times of war." The chief went on to say that such practices were now changing, and Quakers were frequently indistinguishable from others. "If Friends have assumed the war hat, the war coat, and the war speech, how can they be distinguished from the white warriors?" (Minutes, 1826).

The school reopened in late 1826, however, with 16 students in attendance, four others sent to live in the Quaker community of Springfield, Ohio, 70 miles away. The success of the school, farm, and mills necessitated hiring more staff and brought increased expenses. All the funds available for support were overextended, and for a time it appeared that the school would have to be suspended again, but assurances were received from Baltimore that the work could continue, and it did into 1828.

Final Challenges and the End of the Work in Ohio

However, in the fall of 1828 the Hicksite/Orthodox separation occurred in Baltimore Yearly Meeting. While the work at Wapakoneta remained in the hands of the Orthodox branch of Ohio and Indiana Yearly Meeting, the Hicksites retained control of the Indian fund in Baltimore. The school closed until mid-1829 and was in session only sporadically for the next few years.

In 1831 the Shawnees were notified by the Indian agent for Ohio that a special United States commissioner would soon arrive to arrange for the sale of their lands. Such an occasion was inevitable following the passage in 1830 of the Indian Removal Act. After a two-week consultation with the commissioner, a final agreement was made, and a treaty was signed -- after the commissioner discouraged the Indians from reading the long document. Almost immediately, the Indians became aware that they had been deceived in the terms of the agreement.

In company with four Shawnee chiefs, two Quakers from Ohio Yearly Meeting in December of 1831 traveled to Washington, D.C. to represent the Indians' concerns. The delegation met with Secretary of War Lewis Cass and compared the notes Quakers had taken at the treaty council with the terms of the actual agreement. Cass agreed that the Indians had been cheated and promised additional compensation. When presented with the proposal, however, President Andrew Jackson refused, so the delegation approached Congress through an Ohio Representative, Joseph Vance. Eventually, the visit bore some fruit, with increased compensation -- though only one-third of that requested -- given the Indians.

Anticipating removal, the Shawnees at Wapakoneta sold their herds in the winter of 1832: 200 cattle and 1,200 hogs. But then their departure was delayed until fall. Destitute, they turned to Friends for assistance. Provisions were provided both from the superintendent's establishment and from aid gathered from other Quaker communities. Secretary of War Cass also sent relief supplies.

By the summer of 1833, the Indians at Wapakoneta and other villages in western Ohio had completed their removal to Missouri. The last Quaker staff at the farm and school departed in late 1832, and the Friends' property, exclusive of a small burial ground, was sold to a farmer for $1,200. The Quaker work among the Indians in Ohio had come to a close.

Remaining behind in his beloved Wapakoneta, though, was Chief Black Hoof. He had died in 1831, having been born on the shores of the Atlantic and roamed the extensive Shawnee hunting grounds in the East through his youth and young adulthood, only to live out his last years on a ten square mile reservation with the realization that further dislocation would befall his people. Shortly before his death, he related to the sympathetic Indian agent John Johnston, "We know from past experience you will keep driving us until we reach the sea...and then we must jump off" (Johnston, 1842, p.45).

Conclusion

What is, then, to be made of the Quaker work among the Native Americans of Indiana and Ohio in the early 1800s? Ultimately, their work with them in helping create thriving farms only made the land more attractive to white settlers. Both their work along the Wabash River and at Wapakoneta proved to be of short duration and, eventually, destroyed or sold after Indian removal. They eventually conformed to what Robert Berkhofer describes as the Quaker practice of "seeking to civilize the Indian in order that s/he might be Christianized."

Yet it was the Indians themselves who first invited the Quakers to work with them after their hunting lands began disappearing, trusting Friends to honor their culture while other Christian groups forced conversion on them in return for assistance. Chiefs Little Turtle and Black Hoof both expressed their appreciation for Friends while urging respect for Indian traditions and spirituality, which the Quaker workers basically honored. There was language among some Friends of the "savages" needing the benefits of "civilization," but Friends' work did not include required adoption of the Christian religion, and their farms and buildings were intentionally moved off of the Shawnee reservation lest there be any suspicion of a desire to take over Indian holdings.

As with Quaker anti-slavery work, the efforts were commendable, even if the behavior was not always consistent with later standards and attitudes about race and culture. And isn't that an ongoing question? How do we judge the past by the values and principles of the present? By proving to have had a mixed record in their work among Native Americans in the Midwest, Friends turned out to be, in the end, not that "exceptional," while much of their work can be admired.

Discussion Questions

1. Most Christian "missions" to Native Americans in the 1800s sought to "Christianize" them in order that they might be "civilized." Scholars have observed that Quaker missions more typically sought to "civilize" Indians in order that they might become "Christianized." How might the work in the Midwest be assessed according to these observations?

2. Studies in settler-colonialism emphasize these points:
    a. Settler-colonialism is a structure, not an event.
    b. Settler-colonialism destroys in order to replace.
    c. Settler-colonialism is eliminatory, not necessarily genocidal.
    d. Settler-colonialism assumes indigeneity.
    e. Settler-colonialism legitimizes itself by pointing to "harm reduction."

    How might Quaker work in the Midwest be considered in the light of thinking of Quakers as settlers?

3. What does the record of Friends' work among Native Americans in the Midwest teach us about Quaker "good works" today?

References

Berkhofer Jr., R. (1957) *Salvation and the Savage.* University of Kentucky Press

Harvey, H. (1855). *History of the Shawnee Indians.* Ephraim Morgan & Sons.

Hill, L. U. (1957). *John Johnston and the Indians.* Piqua, Ohio.

Johnston, J. (1842). *Recollections of Sixty Years.* Cist's Miscellany.

Minutes. (n.d). *Minutes of the Baltimore Yearly Meeting Committee on Indian Concerns.* (n.d.) Book A, 61.

Minutes. (1804, October 15). *Minutes of the Baltimore Yearly Meeting Indian Committee.*

Minutes. (1805, February 4). *Minutes of the Baltimore Yearly Meeting Indian Committee.*

Minutes. (1812, January). *Minutes of the Baltimore Yearly Meeting Indian Committee.*

Minutes. (1818, October 11). *Minutes of Ohio Yearly Meeting.*

Minutes. (1821, August 13). *Minutes of the Baltimore Yearly Meeting Indian Committee.*

Minutes. (1826, October 6). *Minutes of the Indiana Indian Committee.*

9 | GENTLE INVADERS
Quaker Women Educators and Race Before, During, and After the Civil War

By Linda B. Selleck

Has God provided for the poor a coarser earth, a thinner air, a paler sky?
Mind is immortal. Mind is imperial. It bears no mark of high or low, of rich or poor.
It heeds no bound of time or place, of rank or circumstance.
It asks but freedom. It requires but light. [1]

During August of 1831 Nat Turner led six other slaves in the most successful slave revolt in American history.[2] Their uprising in Southampton County, Virginia left 51 whites, and up to 14 slaves murdered as they swept across the farmlands. A second bloodbath followed, as Turner and his band were captured and hanged, and over 50 innocent slaves executed. In the aftermath, hundreds more innocent slaves were beaten or tortured.

Educated by his owner, Turner was a forceful preacher who believed his liberating actions divinely supported by the Book of Revelation. All Southern states quickly passed laws prohibiting any kind of schooling for either enslaved or free blacks, with dire consequences to those caught teaching (Selleck, 1995).[3]

---

[1] From a speech given on December 13, 1838 to the US House of Representatives by J. Orville Taylor, *Documents on the Subject of Common Schools, published agreeably to Resolution of Legislature of North Carolina* (Raleigh, NC, Printed by Thos. J. Lemay, 1839), p. 77.

[2] During the South Carolina Stono Rebellion in September 1739, around 150 slaves murdered 20 whites. They headed for Florida, but most were intercepted and killed by local militia. Taken from Peter H. Wood, *Black Majority: Negroes in Colonial South Carolina from 1670 through the Stono Rebellion.* (New York, NY: W. W. Norton & Company, Inc., 1975).

[3] Portions of the contents of this chapter are from my book *Gentle Invaders: Quaker Women Educators and Racial Issues During the Civil War and Reconstruction.* (Richmond, IN: Friends United Press, 1995) and are used by permission of Friends United Press. All rights reserved. Born in Suffolk, Virginia, I grew up in Southampton County. Happy childhood memories exist along with bizarre forms of racism by various residents. When I was in elementary school during a

Notwithstanding the consequences of mutilation and even death, blacks secretly passed on to their children what instruction they could.

As early as the late 1700s, northern Quakers of the Religious Society of Friends had created learning opportunities for people of color, including native Indians, free blacks and slaves.[4] Southern Quakers shared these concerns, but after the 1831 Insurrection, responded with sorrow to Friends' queries regarding the education of their meeting and community children, citing the oppressive laws which blocked full efforts.

Located near Suffolk, Virginia in Nansemond County, Somerton Friends Meeting was established in 1672, and was especially sensitive about race issues as Nansemond bordered Southampton County, which boasted one of the largest slave populations in the American colonies. The Lower Monthly Meetings, which included Somerton Friends, acknowledged in 1860 that the instruction of blacks in learning was much neglected. By 1861 they reported that blacks were instructed in useful learning "except a literary education which is prohibited." In September 1865 their answer read, "More care to instruct [blacks] in useful learning would be best" (Lower Monthly Meeting, 1860, Microfilm Number 814). The limitations faced by Friends regarding black education changed at the close of the Civil War.

Somerton Friends were thus one in mind and spirit when approached by the Freedmen's Bureau situated in Suffolk. With the help of local blacks and the Bureau, they prepared to build and open the first school for the freed people in Nansemond County in January 1866. The decision to open a school was a daunting and potentially dangerous task. Madison Newby, a black Virginian, reported to Congress on the chances of creating black schools in Surry County, which shared a northern border with Southampton County. Newby's testimony to the Congressional Committee on Reconstruction in 1866 stressed certain dangers.

> There are no colored schools down in Surry County; they would kill anyone who would go down there and establish colored schools... Down in my neighborhood they [the blacks] are afraid to be caught with a book (Joint Committee on Reconstruction, 1866, p. 55).

---

school bus ride a boy passed around a shiny, black, leather-like paddle. When I asked what it was, he replied, "It's the skin of that nigger Nat Turner. He got hung and cut up and we got a part of him." Years later I asked my older sister if this memory could be false. She replied, "Nah – those boys brought that stuff to school all the time."

[4] Early Friends embraced the pejorative insult of Quaker, and so over time the two words became interchangeable.

Olive Roberts, a Quaker from New York, agreed to teach and upon arrival at Somerton expected at least 40 students. As the modest one-room school was completed, Roberts affectionately called it her "little knowledge-box" (Selleck, 1995, p.153). The list of students quickly grew. Parents, grandparents, aunts and uncles joined their young ones on evenings and Sundays, eager to learn to write their names and the dates of their births. Some composed letters in hopes of being reunited with loved ones sold away from their families.

Three months later the school and the Quaker meetinghouse[5] lay in ashes, the night work of enraged white neighbors. It would take years to raise the money and purchase materials necessary to rebuild.[6] In a detailed letter that Roberts sent to the *Friends' Review* (1866), it stated that she believed the fire was deliberately set by neighbors who knew that weighty Friends John Cox and William Hare would be away from their homes overnight on business.

On the day after the burning, Roberts met on the grounds with a group of freedmen who promised a new building in ten days if she would continue her work. Roberts poignantly observed that the freed people took their losses very quietly but were more determined than ever to learn (*Friends' Review*, 1866). After significant discernment, the school mission was laid down but still bore fruit. In later years a student of Roberts, Della Irving Hayden, would be lauded as one of the finest black women educators in the South.

Olive Roberts was one of hundreds of northern Quaker women, products of a "guarded" upbringing, who left behind families and meetings, traveling into southern regions working both for and with African Americans during and after the Civil War. Drawing upon centuries of racial awareness, and active testimony against Christians who owned slaves yet claimed a valid faith, these women stretched the boundaries of acceptable public service and aid to free and enslaved blacks. Their radical missions included setting up schools, distributing material aid, and providing medical care when possible.

Wherever they lived and worked, most often these women were despised as Yankee intruders by the white communities, considered the afterguard of the Union Army which had indiscriminately reduced the South to ashes. Practically annihilated by the destruction of war, white Southerners slowly began to rebuild their lives. They did not appreciate nor welcome the humanitarian zeal of these teachers.

---

[5] Friends called their worship buildings meetinghouses, as they understood "Church" to be the people gathered by the Holy Spirit, who loved and served Jesus Christ.
[6] Many Friends Meetings which comprised Virginia Yearly Meeting were laid down in the 1840s due to Quaker migration into slave-free territories. However, Somerton Friends Meeting and a few others joined Baltimore Yearly Meeting. It continues to hold regular Sunday meetings for worship in the same location and is now part of North Carolina Yearly Meeting.

But the work pressed forward. Classes were conducted in all kinds of places – the midst of shanty towns, federal conscription camps, tents along the Mississippi, mule stables, and decaying Southern mansions. Eventually new schools and orphanages were established, equipping untold numbers of students both young and old with lives of increasing knowledge, life skills, purpose, and hope.

Friends were not alone in these ventures. Many Northerners of other church affiliations accepted southern posts. The American Missionary Association supported hundreds of academic and vocational schools, while other denominations set up teaching missions. At the same time African Americans were busy establishing their own schools. Quaker periodicals published information released by the Freedmen's Bureau and Quaker agents who witnessed firsthand the immense efforts of former slaves in securing their children's future. Thousands of dollars were raised to build black schools and hire black teachers, confronting public stereotypes that the freed people were intellectually inferior, incapable of financial management, and in need of the paternalistic guidance of sympathetic whites (Selleck, Western Yearly Meeting Lecture, 1994).

Above all, Quaker women educators desired an active role in the national discourse of addressing and publicizing the grave needs of the freed people struggling to obtain access to educational, political, and economic liberties. Without the ability to read, write, and transact business, their chances for work to acquire basic needs for survival were slim in the intensely competitive and racist environment of the post-bellum South. As almost four million former slaves accepted their new status as American citizens, their desperate needs for political representation and protections became paramount. In addition, in just a few years an estimated one million freed slaves would succumb to disease and starvation following their massive dislocations as a result of emancipation, and the collapse of their former lives (Downs, 2012).

Some Friends women educators had short-term tasks, with finances and oversight provided by Quaker abolitionists. Others stayed until their schools were destroyed and their lives threatened. Many returned north after the financial and protective aid of the Freedmen's Bureau was abruptly halted. A number went eager to serve, only to succumb to deadly southern diseases. And some discovered a noble and mighty vocation, dedicating the rest of their lives to the work. Their stories are preserved through personal letters, diaries, journals, correspondence to Friends meetings and organizations, and minutes noted in Quaker business meeting records.

Following are sketches of some of these bold educational pioneers taken from this author's book *Gentle Invaders: Quaker Women Educators and Racial*

Issues During the Civil War and Reconstruction (Selleck, 1995). A selection of Friends women who strived to teach blacks before the Civil War, at the beginning of the war, and during the time of Reconstruction are included, along with responses to the discomfort of Quakers not prepared to welcome blacks into full church membership. Of these Friends, the decades-long work in Arkansas of Alida and Calvin Clark, members of Indiana Yearly Meeting of Friends, stand out.

Near the close of the Civil War, out of the misery of a slave refugee camp along the Mississippi and the confines of a government mule stable, emerged the most successful and sustained enterprise of black education, race relations, and religious equality achieved by Friends on American soil. Having volunteered to take responsibility for abandoned slave children, within a few decades Alida and Calvin Clark had established Southland College, the first diploma-granting black college west of the Mississippi, along with the first African American Friends Meeting.

The Birth of Southland College

On the Arkansas banks of the Mississippi during the winter of 1864, Union Army General Napoleon Bonaparte Buford had a problem. As his troops advanced southward, lost or orphaned slave children had attached themselves for care and protection to the 56th Colored Infantry, one of the regiments under his command. Buford and his wife were moved by "the sad condition of a large number of colored children . . . suffering greatly from neglect and exposure" (Kennedy, 2009, p.5), so he contacted Indiana Yearly Meeting of Friends in search of a couple willing to travel to Arkansas and establish an orphanage.

Buford's appeal was answered when Friends appointed Alida and Calvin Clark as their agents, who arrived on April 8, 1864. Their families had migrated from North Carolina to Indiana in the early 1800s, where both Calvin and Alida were born in Wayne County. Married in 1844, the Clarks had three daughters, but only Eliza survived into adulthood.

The education of blacks in Quaker communities in Indiana Yearly Meeting, established in 1821, was by this time a long-standing interest. In 1826 a "Committee on the Concerns of the People of Color" was created. In three decades it started over two dozen schools for people of color operated by Friends and staffed mostly by black educators and support workers. Quakers paid teachers' salaries, purchased books and Bibles and aided the sick and destitute. (*Friends' Review*, 1871). University of Arkansas historian Thomas C. Kennedy relates that after meeting with Buford, the Clarks met their sixteen charges described as "ragged, filthy, vermin-infested Negro children, brought . . . in a government wagon drawn by six mules . . . the advance guard of hundreds more" (Kennedy, 2009, p.5). Alida loved to tell the story of the beginnings of their work, for it was born in a humble stable, just like Jesus.

The 56th Colored Infantry, along with the head of their regiment, Prussian emigrant Colonel Charles Bentzoni, desired a permanent situation for the children. From meager earnings, within months the men contributed enough funds to buy thirty acres of land and the raw materials necessary to erect a wooden structure to house the Clarks and children near Helena, Arkansas.

In his writings on Quaker contributions to the Reconstruction of southern states, historian Francis Anscombe described the dramatic dedication of the new quarters.

> The colonel and his regiment marched nine miles to the ceremony, and with cheering planted the Stars and Stripes in front of the building and fired three rounds. A procession was then formed, including the regiment, the managers and teachers, visitors, and the children of the orphanage (Selleck, 1995, p. 194-195).

All proceeded to a nearby grove, where a feast had been readied by the soldiers. Colonel Bentzoni, who considered Alida Clark the "grandest woman" he had ever known, handed the deed of the property over to her, who accepted it on behalf of Indiana Yearly Meeting. Within two years Indiana Quakers purchased an additional fifty acres, and by 1925 had increased the final size of the property to 167 acres.

For the next twenty-two years Calvin managed the property and cultivated the farm, planting thousands of fruit trees along with experimental crops of corn, Irish and sweet potatoes, peas and pumpkins, which all rivaled the surrounding ubiquitous cotton. Alida was simply known as "The Guiding Light," an untiring zealot for the WORK which she always underlined in her voluminous correspondence. Alida's name became internationally familiar, as her letters crisscrossed the United States and the Atlantic, keeping Friends everywhere informed of the work now known as Southland.

Working tirelessly to find permanent homes for the children, as soon as dozens left the Clarks' care dozens more appeared. In Alida's spare time, she began organizing a school. Indiana Yearly Meeting officially named the Clarks superintendent and matron, offices they held until 1886 at retirement. Just a dozen years later the school had evolved by 1876 into the first diploma-granting college for African Americans west of the Mississippi.

Eliza Clark soon joined her parents and quickly gained a reputation as an excellent teacher. She married Union veteran Captain Theodore F. Wright, and they settled permanently in the area, as did her parents. John Henry Douglas, a Friends minister from Iowa, visited in 1865 and observed that Eliza was "a No. 1 teacher for the colored children; she loves them, and they in turn love her, and thereby she is enabled to do whatever she pleases with them" (Selleck, 1995, p. 196). Before departing, Douglas led worship for over 300 of the freed people. He prepared them for a Friends service but encouraged singing if they were led to do so. Douglas's preaching was followed by silent worship and closed with a song. He reported: "It has been said that we cannot make Quakers of these people. I most earnestly say that if we would we can make living Quakers of them… They would be newborn Quakers, or Christians" (Kennedy,1865, p. 36).

Later reports chronicled additional maladies: incest, unmarried mothers, and family violence. Temperance was as pressing a concern as education and by 1883 Southland would boast over 1,000 members in its organization. To Alida's disgust communities wasted so much money on bars and alcohol consumption that no funds were left for schools for either black or white students. Three years into the Clarks' work in Arkansas a cholera outbreak occurred, creating new orphans. Alida increased her correspondence as "the overflow piled people up into heaps." Always included was an appeal for funds. "I do not wish to lose any good thing by not asking for it," she wrote (*Friends' Review*, 1867, p. 715).

Then there were outbreaks of revenge killings and violent attacks. "Our Institution's life and existence are threatened by the "Ku Klux," Alida wrote, "and only saved and prolonged by a fear and dread of insurrection by the blacks" (*Friends' Review*, 1868, p. 157). Reconstruction historians understood the potential of race wars in the wake of escalating hatred, and some believed such uprisings would have resulted in the annihilation of both races.

The work of the Clarks inspired Quaker students from Earlham College in Richmond, Indiana to volunteer as interns and teachers at Southland. During meetings for worship they listened in wonder as spirituals arose out of the silence. Many of the visiting students became professional educators, radically changed in their outlook on racial issues.

It is very likely that Alida and Calvin Clark were emboldened by the radical work and harrowing experiences of Prudence Crandall in the early 1830s. Her attempts to provide schooling in New England to girls of color, followed by outrageous laws and despicable treatment towards Crandall and her students, were reported in the abolitionist paper the *Liberator* and national newspapers. Quaker girls and women admired her commitment and courage in breaking down racial barriers three decades prior to the Civil War, and many prepared themselves to teach.

Prudence Crandall and Her School for Little Misses of Color

In 1831, to the delight of the town residents, Prudence Crandall opened an academy for girls in Canterbury, Connecticut. Soon considered one of the state's best schools, the 28-year old teacher's rigorous curriculum was comparable to that taught in the most prominent schools for boys. The next year Sarah Harris, a 17-year old of mixed white, Native American, and African descent, approached Crandall about becoming a student and was admitted. Outraged parents threatened to withdraw their daughters if Harris continued to attend. In response Crandall closed her school.

Raised a Quaker in Rhode Island, Crandall was educated at the New England Friends Boarding School in Providence, Rhode Island (which operates today as the Moses Brown School) where she studied arithmetic, Latin and science. Although these subjects were not typical for women, Quakers had staunchly believed in equal access to education for both girls and boys since the British movement began in the 1650s (Michals, 2015).

After her school closed, and greatly disturbed by the virulent response from parents, Crandall next sought advice and guidance from several abolitionist friends, including Unitarian minister Samuel J. May, publisher William Lloyd Garrison, and businessman and benefactor Arthur Tappan of New York. The previous year Garrison had begun publication of his abolitionist paper the *Liberator*, and in 1832 helped form the New England Anti-Slavery Society. Arthur Tappan was a financial contributor to many humanitarian causes. In 1831 Tappan's summer home in New Haven, Connecticut was destroyed by a mob (along with a black hotel and a black home) after citizens learned of his financial support for the proposal of a black college in that city (Norman, 2016).

May, Garrison and Tappan met with Crandall to strategize options to challenge not only the racism of the Canterbury inhabitants, but to determine the legal rights of blacks pursuing education in states that had outlawed slavery. Although free blacks were required to pay taxes, they were not American citizens. Thirty-five years later, through a four-step prolonged process, their status changed. The 13th Amendment to the U.S. Constitution, ratified in December 1865, abolished slavery; the Civil Rights Act of 1866 made blacks full U.S. citizens; the 14th Amendment of 1868 granted full citizens out of African Americans and also employed language to prohibit discrimination against all citizens and to ensure equal protection under the law. In 1870 the 15th Amendment extended the right to vote to black males.

Crandall and her friends designed a bold plan. A small advertisement, published in March 1833 in Garrison's *Liberator*, announced the opening of Crandall's boarding school for "Little Misses of Color" in Canterbury, the first such in the state. This new enterprise began with sixteen students. The neighboring church which had allowed local blacks to attend worship, informed Crandall that she and her students were no longer welcome. The Quaker meeting at Black Hill was available but hard to reach, so Sunday devotionals were held privately within the school.

An outrage of insults and barbarities followed. Local boys filled her drinking well with stable refuse and hurled manure chips at Crandall and the girls when they braved public outings, while neighbors refused her drinking water. The town council met to determine how to most effectively destroy Crandall's initiatives, passing hostile ordinances directed at herself, her students, and her Quaker family who received exorbitant fines for hauling water into town for the school's needs.

The local authorities eventually arrested and jailed Crandall on technicalities having to do with transporting blacks across state lines. Her arrest came after authorities passed laws which allowed charges that she "willfully and knowingly did harbor and board certain colored persons [who] were not inhabitants of any town in this state" (Fuller, 1971, p. 6). These actions circumvented the issue of black schooling, as Crandall's enemies seized upon the so-called "Black Law" passed four weeks previously by the state Legislature, in response to a petition presented by Canterbury citizens. They then threatened students with public whippings for failure to pay fines now encased within the new laws (Fuller, 1971).

A newspaper editorial condoned these vicious actions by explaining that Crandall, in initiating her scheme without approval of the town fathers, had "stepped out of the hallowed precincts of female propriety and now stands on common ground, and must expect common treatment" (Strane, 1990, p.84). Crandall again turned to her trusted abolitionist friends for counsel, who helped carefully choreograph her legal defense, with the financial aid of Arthur Tappan. Through the events of three highly publicized trials, Crandall raised the issue of U.S. citizenship status for free black people who payed taxes, and therefore deserved to cross state lines. When the judge and prosecutors realized the direction Crandall and her lawyers were headed, all charges were dismissed.

It was a short-lived victory however, for around midnight on September 9, 1834, Crandall and her students awoke to the sounds of local men and youth, armed with heavy clubs and iron bars, methodically beating down window sashes and smashing ninety panes of glass until no protection was left. Samuel J. May, who had arrived to give Crandall support during the trials, was requested to announce to the twenty remaining students her decision to abandon the work. May recorded his observations of the ordeal:

I was summoned next morning to the scene of destruction and the ter-ror-stricken family. Never before had Miss Crandall seemed to quail, and her pupils had become afraid to remain another night under her roof . . . because, forsooth, the house in which they dwelt would not be protected by the guardians of the town, the conservators of the peace, the officers of justice, the men of influence in the village where it was situated. . . . I felt ashamed of Canterbury, ashamed of Connecticut, ashamed of my country, ashamed of my color. Thus ended the gener-ous, disinterested, philanthropic, Christian enterprise of Prudence Cran-dall (May, 1968, p.71).

Later that year Crandall married Baptist minister Calvin Philleo and continued her advocacy for blacks. In 1886, an annual pension of $400 was given her by the Connecticut Legislature until her death in 1890. Through the initiating efforts of school children, Crandall was designated Connecticut's state heroine in 1995 (Encyclopedia Britannica, 2020).

Crandall's fortitude forever changed Sarah Harris, and two of her daughters became teachers in Southern states. "Little Miss of Color" Elizabeth Smith became a teacher in Rhode Island. Julia Williams soon moved to New Hampshire and studied at an integrated school until August 10, 1835 when hun-dreds of armed white men appeared. After three days of diligent labor, they man-aged with the help of yokes of oxen to drag the main building off the school property and deposit it in a nearby swamp (Encyclopedia Britannica, 2020).

Prudence Crandall's highly publicized struggles attracted a new wave of Quaker women teachers willing to risk life and reputation to help empower blacks. Laura M. Towne was one such Friend affected by reports of Quaker-sponsored schools for black people, and the resulting increase for the common good in those communities.

Laura Towne and the Penn School

After the Union Army capture of Port Royal, South Carolina in No-vember 1861, the U.S. government advertised for agents to travel to the Sea Is-lands to aid contraband refugee relief. Here the first Union movement in Recon-struction commenced, and here the test was most severe. Volunteer Laura Ma-tilda Towne arrived at St. Helena with instructions to oversee the distribution of a large store of provisions for thousands of contrabands on the Sea Islands. Two days after her arrival in April 1862, Towne complained in her journal that a too cautious spirit prevailed among the northern workers. "I wish they would all say out loud quietly, respectfully, firmly, 'We have come to do anti-slavery work, and we think it noble work and we mean to do it earnestly'" (Holland, 1912, p. 8).

A Quaker with Unitarian leanings, Laura was soon joined by Ellen Murray, also a Friend. After surviving a hot, muggy, insect-ridden summer, together in September of 1862 they opened the state's first school for blacks, albeit contrabands. Initially Towne and Murray met with nine students at The Oaks Plantation, and when the enrollment increased to 132 they relocated to the Brick Baptist Church on St. Helena Island. Built by slave labor in 1855, their owners sat on the lower level of its spacious sanctuary, while in the upper balcony slaves stood out of view. After the war, the U.S. government sold abandoned plantations and land holdings to the freedmen. The Brick Baptist Church was turned over to former slaves as their house of worship, and soon had over 1,000 members (Brick Baptist Church, 2020).[7]

Other women joined Towne and Murray in their work, then moved on to establish schools of their own. The first black woman to teach at the Penn School was Charlotte Forten, who stayed through 1864. Raised in a wealthy, influential black Philadelphia home, she knew many in the Friends community and maintained a life-long correspondence with Quaker poet and abolitionist John Greenleaf Whittier. Writing in 1864, Whittier reminded Friends that:

> We have to undo the accumulated wrongs of two centuries, remake the manhood that slavery has well-nigh unmade, to see to it that the long oppressed colored man has a fair field for development and improvement, and to tread under our feet the last vestige of that hateful prejudice which has been the strongest external support of Southern slavery (Kennedy, 2009, p.18).

Contraband was "just another word for government slave," Towne bitterly observed, as the slaves were put to hard labor cultivating cash crops by the soldiers, who then pocketed the profits. Many starved as the Union soldiers refused them the necessary time to plant gardens for the survival of the workers and their families. At first Towne and Murray lived in a deserted plantation home, taking their meals in the formal dining room which came equipped with a whipping post and stretching pulleys, evidence of the force required to maintain the institution of slavery. The soldiers often brutalized the contrabands, and on one occasion Towne managed to intercept, report, and halt the fraudulent sale of slaves by a Union officer.

After her first day of teaching, Towne described in her diary the behavior of her eighty scholars.

---

[7] The church continues to minister to the people on St. Helena Island. Their website has this Bible verse at the top of the masthead: *"Upon this rock I will build my church, and the gates of hell shall not prevail against it." Matthew 16:18.*

They had no idea of sitting still, of giving attention, of ceasing to talk aloud. They lay down and went to sleep, they scuffled and struck each other. They got up by the dozen, made their curtsies, and walked off to the neighboring field for blackberries, coming back to their seats with a curtsy when they were ready. They evidently did not understand me, and I could not understand them, and after two hours and a half of effort I was thoroughly exhausted (Holland, 1912, p. xv).

Towne named her school for William Penn, Quaker founder of Pennsylvania and champion of religious and human liberties. Along with teaching, she provided medical care, having trained under Dr. Constantine Hering of the Female Medical College of Pennsylvania (now the Medical College of Pennsylvania). Founded in 1850 by Philadelphia Quakers, it was the first in the country to train women as physicians. During 1862 Towne battled smallpox and yellow fever, reporting on the deaths of several teachers and others who returned north to recover their health. Although the Penn School provided the first official education to blacks, there is no way to determine how much illicit learning was passed on from slaves who had obtained some education. Will Capers, an ex-slave cabinet maker, informed Laura Towne that he had operated a secret night school for male slaves for years (Holland, 1912).

Towne and Murray provided education and friendship to the black community for over forty years, as Penn graduates went on to serve and elevate their race as teachers, ministers, lawyers and physicians. Towne continued providing medical skills and school oversight until her death in 1901. Her last diary entry reported a "visit" in 1884 while she was sitting with a book on the sunny verandah of her home. A North Penn Railroad conductor informed her that:

> The whole race of niggers ought to be swept away, and I told him my business was with that race and that they would never be swept away, so he was disgusted and went away, leaving me to read in peace" (Holland, 1912, p. 310).[10]

---

[10] Eventually the school was transferred to Hampton Institute, but its presence continues as the Penn Center, which is used as a retreat site, and in the 1960s hosted a gathering headed by Dr. Martin Luther King.

Black Women Educators Emerge

Harriet Brent Jacobs

Harriet Brent Jacobs, who insisted she was not a commodity to be bought or sold, became a teacher, nurse, writer, and abolitionist speaker. She was born a slave in 1813 and orphaned at age six when her mother died. The daughter of Jacobs' new owner taught her to sew, read and write. At the age of twelve Jacobs was inherited by Dr. James Norcom's three-year old daughter. As Jacobs matured her life became almost unbearable, as Norcom sexually harassed her for years. Determined to keep Norcom at arms' length, and to commit to a man worthy of her affections, Jacobs gave her love and friendship to Samuel Sawyer, a white lawyer who years later became a member of the U.S. House of Representatives. Sawyer was the father of Jacobs' only two children, Joseph and Louisa Matilda.

Norcom continued his advances upon Jacobs, threatening to keep her, but sell her children to separate owners as field workers. Fearful for their safety, Jacobs hid in the crawl space of her grandmother's home, which measured nine feet by seven feet, with its highest point at three feet. Seven years passed as Jacobs sewed clothing for her children and listened to their voices at play. In 1842 Jacobs escaped by ship and was given sanctuary by northern Quakers, who obtained her freedom papers and supported her teaching. They also helped Jacobs purchase her two children, who joined her in the North.

With New York Quaker Amy Post's encouragement, Jacobs published her autobiography, *Incidents in the Life of a Slave Girl*, the first authored by a black woman. With sorrow she declared there were no bonds as strong as those formed by shared suffering (Brent, 1861).[11] After the war Jacobs noted the great stir caused when a white Baptist Church invited blacks to worship in her birthplace of Edenton, North Carolina. In a letter to Edna Dow Cheney, Jacobs writes: "The Churches have been open night and day [now] these people have time to think of their souls, [as] now they are not compelled to think for the Negro" (Jacobs, Letter to Edna Dow Cheney, 1867).

Editors of *The Freedmen's Record* printed an update on Jacobs in December 1868. Having taught school in Alexandria, Virginia for three years, Jacobs returned to her childhood home of Edenton where she came across the son of her former owner. He professed to have no property, to have served in the Union Army during the war, and to have been a good friend to the Negro. He won-

---

[11] *Incidents in the Life of a Slave Girl* was written by Harriet Brent Jacobs under the pseudonym Linda Brent.

dered with Jacobs' influence if she could help him procure work with the Freedmen's Bureau. The editors described this ironic encounter as another example of the world turned upside down (*The Freedmen's Record*, 1865).

Mary Jane Patterson and Fanny Jackson Coppin

The first two black women to obtain full college degrees both graduated from Oberlin College in Ohio: Mary Jane Patterson in 1862 and Fanny Jackson Coppin in 1865. Patterson and Coppin were hired as teachers by Quakers after their graduation. In his history of Oberlin College, Robert Samuel Fletcher speculated that Patterson, born in Raleigh, North Carolina, was brought to Oberlin as a child by her parents, who were probably fugitive slaves (Fletcher, 1943). Coppin, born a slave in Washington, D.C. but eventually purchased by a relative, was supporting herself by the age of 14 as a domestic servant. Saving her money, Coppin eventually made her way to Oberlin College, arriving with a passion to educate her own race. In her autobiography, Coppin wrote:

> When I was within a year of graduation, an application came from a Friends' school in Philadelphia for a colored woman who could teach Greek, Latin, and higher mathematics. The answer returned was: "We have the woman, but you must wait a year for her." Then began a correspondence with Alfred Cope,[12] a saintly character, who, having found out what my work in college was, teaching my classes in college, besides sixteen private music scholars, and keeping up my work in the senior class, immediately sent me a check for eighty dollars [around $1,300 in today's currency], which wonderfully lightened my burden as a poor student (Coppin, 1913, p. 13).

Patterson and Coppin served as Principal and Assistant Principal of the Institute for Colored Youth, established in 1837 by Quakers in Philadelphia (and today known as Cheney University). In 1869 Patterson went to Washington to teach, and Coppin became the head Principal of the Institute, educating two generations of students. Patterson in 1871 became the first principal of the newly established Preparatory High School for Negroes in Washington, D.C. She served until 1884, when an African American man was appointed principal. Patterson continued to teach at the high school until her death in 1894 (Fletcher, 1943).

---

[12] Philadelphia Quaker Alfred Cope and his brother ran a shipping line between Philadelphia and Liverpool, England. In 1849 Cope and Thomas Wister carried $40,000 in gold to Green Bay, Wisconsin for the relief of native American Indians. Cope was a patron of the Cheyney Training School (originally the Institute for Colored Youth). From "Alfred Cope" article through web.tricolib.brynmawr.edu.

Sarah Frances Smiley Visits Somerton Friends School for the Freed People

Raised in Maine, Smiley became a convinced Friend and recorded minister. She carried a burden for Quakers along the Eastern Seaboard as warfare ravaged homes and meetinghouses. Traveling through Virginia and North Carolina after state roads and train lines opened, Smiley encouraged Friends and distributed material goods. Raising the needed funds, she stocked each surviving Friends Meeting after the Civil War with a library of one hundred leather bound Quaker classics and Bibles.

Maintaining a teacher's home in Richmond, Virginia, Smiley started dozens of industrial schools for freedwomen who then taught their skills to the next generation. She was affected deeply by the words of Mary Mason Lyon, a Massachusetts educator who established Wheaton and Mount Holyoke Female Seminaries: "There is but *one* thing I fear, that I shall not *know* and *do* all my duty" (*Friends' Review*, 1866, p. 459-460).

Smiley met with Somerton Friends in Virginia in January 1866, leaving them a set of Quaker books. In his *Journal*, British founder of the Quaker movement George Fox wrote of his several passings in 1672 through "Nancemum," "Sommertown," and the Great Dismal Swamp during his treks through the "cruel bogs" of Virginia, and noted the good worship at the home of John Porter, believed to be an original founder of the Somerton Meeting (Lasley, p. ix.). Smiley was on hand for the opening of the Somerton Friends' school and observed that teacher Olive Roberts kept excellent discipline, that her students had already made good progress, and that Roberts greatly enjoyed her work. Non-Quaker neighbors responded with intense resentment. Albert Jones, born a slave in Southampton County, recalled his owner usually treated him well, but if blacks were caught with a book or paper, or praising God, beatings would surely follow (Perdue, C., Barden, T., Phillips, K., 1980).

During her stay at Somerton, Smiley preached to Friends, students and their families. Quaker John Cox told her about an elderly black man Cox met one Sunday evening seven miles from the meetinghouse, who exuberantly relayed the impact of Smiley's ministry.

> There's a lady thar a opening' of the Scripturs an a unfoldin' of mysteries of things we never thought of in our lives, and it 'pears like I don't know how to surrender tanks enough to the Lord for such a privilege (*Friends' Review*, 1866, p. 478.

Three months later, the meetinghouse and the school were burned down, halting the education of the 114 students now attending. The destruction was one piece of bad news joining many others, as the burnings of meetinghouses and school buildings grew in number. Baltimore Quakers pondered the effects of their educational activities, as eleven buildings used by the Association for black education had recently been burned and one teacher had been shot, the bullet fortunately passing through his coat (*Friends' Review*, 1866). English Quaker J. J. Neave wrote to William H. Hare, a weighty Friend who was away from the Somerton area when the school and meetinghouse were destroyed.

> The setting fire to your Meeting House shows that the spirit of evil still lives in the breasts of some of the pro-slavery party; may their eyes be opened to see their sin and folly that so they may be turned from spiteful incendiarys [*sic*] to good neighbors (Lasley, 1972, p. ix.).

Later that year the query concerning instruction of slaves and Africans under the care of Friends was dropped. In 1867 Query No. 8 now read: "We believe friends bear a faithful testimony against oaths, military services, clandestine-trade prize goods, lotteries and slavery and none of the African race are under our immediate care" (Lower Monthly Meeting Minutes, 1867, Microfilm, 814).

Two years later Somerton Friends rebuilt their meetinghouse, resuming worship which has continued to the present day. About three miles from the location, an historical marker was placed on U.S. Highway 58 on July 4, 2016 stating that "The Somerton Meetinghouse, along with a nearby school for African Americans, was burned in 1866. The congregation constructed its current building on the same site in 1869" (MacCaulay, 2016, paragraph 6). They still have some leather-bound books from Smiley.

The brief period of Olive Robert's work however produced surprising results. Former student Cornelia Copeland, still living in the Somerton community in 1924, was known as an excellent writer. During her lifetime Copeland taught hundreds of black people to read and write (Anscombe, 1926). And then there was Della Irving Hayden, whose commitment to black education raised teaching standards and received admiring praise across the South.

Della Irving Hayden

Raised in North Carolina by her grandmother, at age fifteen Hayden rejoined her mother in Virginia and began studies at the Somerton Friends school. After its destruction, Hayden found ways to continue her education, despite study interruptions and limited finances. Within ten years she graduated with honors from the Hampton Normal and Industrial Institute, with Booker T. Washington as a fellow classmate.

Hayden served as principal of the Virginia Normal and Industrial Institute in Petersburg, Virginia for thirteen years. She then organized and was principal of the Franklin, Virginia Normal and Industrial Institute in 1904. Within twelve years Hayden had solicited enough money for improvements and acquisitions that the Institute had buildings, land to operate a small farm, and space to board dozens of women students. She wrote, "I have been trying to teach my people to help themselves. It has been my heart's desire to help elevate my race" (Monahan, 1993, paragraph 1).

Hayden served with distinction as a beloved and respected spiritual and educational leader, and political advisor to the black community until her death in 1924. Historian Monroe A. Majors, M.D. wrote, "A race, no less than a nation, is prosperous in proportion to the intelligence of its women" (Majors, 1893, Title Page). In his book *Noted Negro Women*, Majors said of Hayden:

> She stands in the ranks among the best educators of her race. Through her influence and recommendations, a great many young men and women have gained admission to some of the best institutions of learning in the United States (Majors, 1893, p.35).

In 1953 the Virginia government built a new high school for black students in Franklin and named it Hayden High School in Della's memory. Sixty-six years later a state historical marker was placed in Franklin in 2019 in commemoration of Hayden and her outstanding achievements.

Spiritual Equality for African Americans at Southland College

The labors of Alida and Calvin Clark at Southland College in Arkansas had produced extraordinary results by the 1870s. Hundreds of former slave children had received shelter and formal schooling. The school residents met for regular worship, but Alida wanted more. She desired spiritual equality for her community in the Religious Society of Friends. Indiana Yearly Meeting had instructed its field workers to gather refugees for worship, and when possible establish permanent worship groups. They were not prepared for Alida's evangelical efforts. She longed for Friends to recognize the freed people as kindred souls. As the Clarks were members of Whitewater Friends Meeting (part of Indiana Yearly Meeting), in 1867 they petitioned Whitewater Friends to enroll around seventy African Americans as members.

Whitewater Friends delayed the request with cautious language and a concern for right order. Defending the enrollments, Alida noted the great distances traveled on foot just to attend worship. She questioned whether Friends had become too adjusted to a life of ease to identify with the spirit of religious awakening. After a lengthy time of discernment, Whitewater Friends accepted seven Southland blacks into membership in 1868, and eight more the next year.

Alida's request caused enough apprehension that future considerations of black membership were sent to the newly formed Missionary Board, which replaced the Freedmen's Committee. Not content with the prospect of black Quaker worship under the oversight of white Friends, the following year the Clarks surprised the Executive Committee with a recommendation to record ex-slave Daniel Drew, a field worker and veteran of the 56th Infantry, as a Friends minister. A new hot topic was forced upon the Board's agenda.

The Clarks had long observed Drew's extraordinary spiritual gifts. While acknowledging the sober weight of the decision, they believed that "the cause of truth will be advanced thereby and . . . way opened for more effectual service among (Christ's) poor people" (Selleck, 1995, p. 206). The Missionary Board considered the matter for two years, while receiving regular letters of glowing praise from Alida for Drew's effective and sincere ministry. Indiana Friends decided in 1870 to establish a preparative meeting called Southland Friends, with 30 charter members. Three months later Daniel Drew became a Friends minister, and Alida Clark's recording in ministry soon followed. Alida shared her frustrations about Quakers and race with *Friends' Review* readers:

> Many *good* people profess to believe that the *colored people* are too emotional and impressible ever to become Friends. . . . A thorough and deep work of grace is just the same in the heart, no matter the color of the skin. . . . is [there] not a prejudice and jealousy (cruel as the grave) against color that is hindering our ultimate success, in doing all the good we desire among them, profiting the present generation, and reaching down to posterity (*Friends' Review*, 1871, p. 763)?

Southland Friends Meeting was given full status in 1873, reporting 78 members on its rolls. Over the next five decades over 560 African Americans received membership, and at least eleven black men became recorded ministers of the Gospel of Jesus Christ. Ten years later Alida was still publishing the fruits of Drew's ministries, often likening his efforts to those of George Fox. A London-based Quaker publication noted her description of Drew as "our main nursing father, as well as minister and evangelist" (*The Friend*, 1883, p. 209).

Alida believed many Friends' hesitation in welcoming blacks into meetings, or organizing separate black meetings for worship, was latent racism. Whenever possible she traveled east, sharing Southland's stories and making financial appeals. One such trip took her to Nashville, Tennessee in 1871, where Alida attended an integrated worship service at Fisk University, then pondered denominational advances in race relations over and against the Quakers. Standing with an assembly of black and white Presbyterians, Methodists, and Congregationalists, Alida wondered why Friends were not intentional in sending out ministers to organize African American worship services. "The more I revolved the subject the more of an unaccountable mystery it seemed, as it always has, to me" (*Friends' Review*, 1868, p. 157).

But when Alida advanced the idea of the rise of black Quaker meetings, Friends imagined the prospect of excitable worship styles accompanied by emotional shouting and singing. In a startling letter to the Executive Board of Friends in Philadelphia dated June 21, 1871, Alida challenged Quaker prejudices.

> What! The followers of Woolman, who is now being afresh declared the first white man to intercede for the freedom of Afric's sons and daughters, the very last to send out ministers, evangelists, etc., to organize meetings and receive into fellowship these sable fellow beings?

> … I think it is time for the Quakers, the acknowledged friends of the red and the black man, to wake up and arouse themselves everywhere to an aggressive movement. If our system of worship is unsuited to the lowly, let it be altered (*Friends' Review*, 1871, p. 759).

What impulses drove Alida Clark to persevere with this difficult, exhausting, and at times life threatening work? What sustained her evangelical fervor, motivating her to prod Indiana Friends into establishing a Friends Meeting at Southland, receiving blacks into full membership, leadership, and pastoral ministry?

Quaker Foundational Beliefs and Actions Towards Equality

First generation Friends held a radical interpretation of New Testament equality, stressing that through spiritual baptism into Christ, men and women could be equal partners in public ministry. They both were part of the new Adam and Eve through the Resurrection. Women were capable of responding to and acting upon the Holy Spirit's leadings, and in receiving any of the spiritual gifts defined in scriptures. The corporate sin would be to deny women the opportunity to both act upon their convictions and exercise their recognized gifts. Early Quaker men and women traveled together and separately throughout the British Isles, Europe and across the Atlantic and Caribbean seas. They proclaimed the Gospel, published Truth, and suffered persecution for their beliefs. Quaker Mary Dyer, hanged on Boston Common in 1660, was the first English woman martyred for religious freedom in the New World.

George Fox wrote an epistle in 1657 addressed to "Friends Beyond Sea, that Have Blacks and Indian Slaves," in which he set forth scriptural support for the equality of all humans in the eyes of God. He organized schools for both girls and boys, so none would grow up ignorant of the scriptures, and published his Catechism for Children in 1660. Fox sent an epistle to the Governor of Barbados in 1671, addressing a concern for the education of people of color.

> We do declare that we esteem it a Duty incumbent on us to Pray with and for, to Teach, Instruct, and Admonish those in and belonging to our Families; this being a command of the Lord. . . . Now Negroes, Tawnies, Indians, make up a very great part of the Families in this Island, for whom an Account will be required by Him, who comes to Judge both Quick and Dead at the great Day of Judgement (Fox, 1986, p. 605-606).

Against much opposition, Fox initiated business meetings led by and for women. Quaker women's meetings were the only formal organizations in the colonies run by women of any religious or political persuasion until the late 1700s. Maryland Quaker women organized the first women's yearly meeting in 1677, and expressed a concern that the children of Friends be educated in regard to justice for "Africans and their posterity formerly in slavery" (Bacon, 1986, p.49).

Quakers were slow to act upon Fox's conviction that Friends should set all of their slaves free, after some instruction and preparation. During the mid-1700s American Friends John Woolman and Anthony Benezet traveled in earnest appeal for across-the-board manumission and by 1797, under the prodding of Benezet, Philadelphia Quakers were supporting seven schools with free tuition for blacks. By 1800 Quakers were operating black schools in New York, North Carolina, Pennsylvania and Virginia. Women ministers acted upon these concerns also. In 1788 Sarah Harrison labored with Friends meetings from Philadelphia to Virginia. The mother of ten, she was responsible for the freeing of two hundred slaves. In one situation alone, fifty slaves were released by their Blackwater, Virginia owners after spending time in prayer with Harrison (Bacon, 1986).

The Religious Society of Friends, which did not divide into northern and southern denominations over slavery, was an anomaly in contrast with other Protestants. Friends, who took seriously the charge of caring for family, friends and neighbors, never sought to proselytize just to increase numbers. In 1840 the U.S. Census posted membership for both Quakers and Methodists at around

40,000. Yet most Friends were uncomfortable with the idea of intentional evangelization – a significant departure from the sacrificial zeal of the first generation. Special Friends services with both African Americans and whites present for worship were reported from time to time, but there was never an effort to create integrated or separate meetings.

Southland Friends Meeting's Effects on the Surrounding Community

Still seeking her elusive endowment, in 1879 at the age of fifty-six Alida Clark took an extensive leave of absence for seven months. She journeyed 7,000 miles, attended over 400 meetings for worship, and raised $3,000 for Southland (around $77,600 in today's currency). She visited women's prisons, black orphanages and schools, and attended Indiana, Philadelphia, and Baltimore Yearly Meeting sessions. Alida insisted she could raise an endowment for Southland if only spared the time to go for it. With the demise of the school 45 years later due greatly to financial shortages, Alida's dream remained tragically unfulfilled.

Quakers Joel Bean and Isaac Sharp visited Southland College on December 21, 1883 for a week. Reporting to *The British Friend*, Bean described their journey from Helena to the school compound, depicting it as the most attractive place he had seen in Arkansas.

> We now see a well-conducted household, a well-ordered school, and a good-sized meeting. . . . We have attended their Meetings for Worship, where the silence seemed sweet and refreshing, and the word preached found place in tender and receptive hearts. We have attended their Monthly Meeting, in which the interest and importance of the subjects considered, the dignity of the proceedings, the variety and force of the remarks made, would compare favourably with our Monthly Meetings in the North. A minister (coloured) returned a minute for service among their scattered members. . . . He spoke of them as maintaining generally, in their isolation and destitution of religious privileges, a Christian life and character which is a light in their respective neighbourhoods... however our Friends in other places might differ with regard to the manner in which some means are employed, such as singing and music, this institution is a Beacon in Arkansas, and an untold blessing to those who have been brought under its influence (Bean, 1883, p. 34).

Friends beyond Southland might not have known that Alida Clark directed a choir.[13] Former student Duncan Freeland recalled traveling with the choir and "Mis' Clark" in a wagon with an old pump organ in the back. Visiting churches that had no music, the choir would sing and Alida would speak on spiritual matters and the need for temperance. Freeland's older son attended Southland and eventually became a physician (Selleck, 1995).

Two years later a female graduate was chosen to give the 1885 commencement address. "Despite the increase of male ministers [it was] the greatest sermon that it has been our privilege ever to hear," Clark contended, noting in a sideways manner the absence of recorded black women ministers at Southland.[14] Entitled "Employments for Women," it detailed the not-too-bright future of her contemporaries, even those with a hard-won education. Alida's coverage in the *Friends' Review* recounted the refined and eloquent delivery and captivated audience, as the young unnamed woman described the "evils and hardships of the Freedwoman."

> Her helplessness to educate and fit herself intelligently for life's duties, and usefulness in the world; her abject slavery often in the marriage relation to ignorant, cruel and domineering husbands, who said little now against oppressions and slavery, since it was theirs to do all the *flogging* themselves without interference of *master or overseer*; subjected to daily *field* labor alongside the man, besides her household, indoor work and care of her children, she was dragging out a life of hopeless servitude and poverty (*Friends' Review*, 1885, p. 46).

Alida ached for these students on the verge of adulthood, who had caught glimpses of a world beyond physical drudgery. She chafed at the slowness of Quakers and society to utilize the talents of graduates capable and eager to work, and hurled her forceful admonitions at Friends:

> One is teaching the "*Free school*"... with 200 enrolled, another of our *girls* assisting her... there are 50 more children to come in, and another assistant – all girls, proving to the *men*, that *women* are their *equals*, and when allowed a chance their *superiors*. There is no more *needed* lesson to be taught them, and well *rubbed in* on them (*Friends' Review*, 1885, p. 45-47).

---

[13] Early Friends sang unaccompanied hymns during worship. George Fox sang hymns in his prison cells. After the 17th century imprisonment of thousands of British Quakers, 18th century Quakers pressed on, but singing faded from worship.
[14] Of the 1871 – 1903 list of Southland's 14 recorded Friends ministers, 11 were African American men. Also recorded were Alida Clark, and teachers Amasa and Lydia Chase, who left Kansas and joined the staff in 1874. Their son also taught at Southland after college.

Years of hardships, frustrations, endless work, and shortages of funds had opened the spiritual eyes of Clark to the next challenge of the Religious Society of Friends and all Americans – the pernicious obstacle of sexism.

Internal discord within Indiana Yearly Meeting, financial tensions, and a string of management complaints against the Clarks prompted their resignation from Southland in the mid-1880s. All charges were investigated and found groundless. But the incensed Clarks had heard enough. In all their years of labor, neither had accepted a salary (*Friends' Review*, 1886). Removing themselves from further character damage, they retired to their farm home two miles away and watched as a succession of short-term managers followed.

When complex factors brought about the closing of the college in 1925, Southland's graduates, now teachers, ministers, and physicians, fanned out across the South, improving and elevating the quality of life for their race, and organizing several preparative black Quaker meetings. Ultimately the college's closing was due to insufficient operating funds, as Quakers struggled to adjust to post-World War I economic distresses. After six decades of uninterrupted service Southland College, with its student body of 135, closed on June 2, 1925. The property was worth $60,000 (around $887,000 in today's currency), and its library held over 1,000 volumes. Southland was sold to the African Methodist Episcopal Church, which hoped to continue its legacy of black education. But the college's isolated location and the opening of another black institution closer to Helena, Arkansas presented insurmountable challenges.

Southland Friends Meeting was also laid down, dissolving both the preparative black Friends meetings and Alida Clark's dreams of great black yearly meetings spread across the south. Even if many white Christians had been willing to consider integrated fellowships, the "Jim Crow" laws passed in the mid-1890s made this choice virtually impossible. Despite the promise of equal protections in the 15th Amendment, "Jim Crow" severely restricted the ability of African Americans to acquire work, travel safely from state to state, and succeed in business. The survival of their race depended upon tightly interconnected personal, spiritual, financial, and geographical relationships.

After two decades in Arkansas, Alida Clark wrote that "only three white women in this Southern land have ever given me a friendly shake of the hand, or an invitation to their homes, or noticed me (Kennedy, p. 29)." Surrounded by her family, Quaker visitors, and the life-long friendships made with her students and their families, Alida continued to preach and write until her death in 1892 at the age of 70, and her beloved Calvin passed away four years later. Of all the Friends who sacrificed and persevered to aid the freed people, none combined the passion for evangelism and the advancement of the mind as did this faithful

Friend, who set upon her tasks with sincerity of soul and conscientious energy, alongside her husband Calvin's unflagging labors, support, and encouragement.

Surely Alida Clark, along with all Friends women educators who strived to equip, educate, support, and befriend 19th century African Americans, significantly aided the cause of peace in a troubled land.

Discussion Questions

1. In the mid-1600s, the early Friends movement was sustained and grew through a radical understanding and experience of the immediacy of the Living Christ. A basic tenet was the trust that spiritual gifts were bestowed upon both women and men through the power of the Holy Spirit, and given to edify, exhort and comfort the church. Friends drew upon Galatians 3:28 for daily renewal: "There is neither Jew nor Gentile, neither slave nor free, nor is there male and female, for you are all one in Christ Jesus." How might Friends' conviction in this verse have strengthened the resolve of these women educators in difficult and hostile surroundings?

2. Friends in the 17th century who traveled around the British Isles and other countries proclaiming Truth, often suffered severe deprivations, persecution, cruel punishments, imprisonment, and sometimes death. Both women and men accepted these potential hazards as consequences of their obedience to the call of the Holy Spirit. How did these women educators persevere and push through their own harsh realities, while proclaiming the equality of all races?

3. If Indiana Yearly Meeting had not replaced the Committee for the Concerns of the People of Color with a Missionary Board, might race relations and the eventual increase of more people of color into Friends membership have occurred?

4. Following the Civil War, if American Friends had captured Alida Clark's vision of releasing Friends ministers to gather up great black yearly meetings across the land, how might race relations have improved, and the history of American Friends been altered? What forces would have hampered a concerted effort to achieve Clark's vision?

References

Anscombe, F. A. (1926). *The contribution of the Quakers to the Reconstruction of the Southern States* (Unpublished doctoral dissertation). University of North Carolina, Chapel Hill, North Carolina.

Bacon, M. H. (1986). *Mothers of feminism: The story of Quaker women in America.* Harper & Row.

Bean, J. (1883, February 1). Joel Bean in Helena, Arkansas. *The British Friend Vol. XLI, No. 2.*

Brent Jacobs, H. (Linda Brent, pseud.). (1861). *Incidents in the life of a slave girl.* (Child, L., Ed). Boston Eleotype Foundry.

Brent Jacobs, H. (1867). Letter to Edna Cheney. Smith Collection: New England Hospital Records. Massachusetts.

Brick Baptist Church (2020, February 12). *Brick Baptist Church 2005, Brick Baptist Church: A historic landmark.* Brick Baptist Church. from www.brickbaptist.com.

Downs, J. (2012). *Sick from freedom: African American illness and suffering during the Civil War and Reconstruction.* Oxford University Press, Inc.

Editors of Encyclopedia Britannica (2020). "Prudence Crandall." Encyclopedia Britannica. Retrieved on February 15, 20202 from https://www.britannica.com/biography/Prudence-Crandall.

Fletcher, R. S. (1943). *A history of Oberlin College -- from its foundation through the Civil War, Volume II.* Oberlin College.

Fox, G. (1986). *Journal of George Fox.* (Nickalls, J. L., Ed.) Religious Society of Friends.

Friends' Review (1866, March 24). *Friends Review, 19.*

Friends' Review (1868, October 31). *Friends Review, 22.*

Friends' Review (1871, July 22). *Friends Review, 24.*

Friends' Review (1885, August 22). *Friends Review, 34.*

Friends' Review (1886, August 26). *Friends Review, 40.*

Fuller, E. (1971). *Prudence Crandall: An incident of racism in nineteenth-century Connecticut.* Wesleyan University Press.

Holland, R. S. (1912). *Letters and diary of Laura M. Towne: Written from the Sea Islands of South Carolina.* Cambridge.

Jackson Coppin, F. (1913). *Reminiscences of school life, and hints on teaching.* Philadelphia, PA.

Joint Committee on Reconstruction (1866). *Report of the Joint Committee on Reconstruction.* Government Printing Office.

Kennedy, T. C. (2009). *A history of Southland College: The Society of Friends and black education in Arkansas.* The University of Arkansas Press.

Lasley, E. H. (1972). *Somerton Meeting: three hundred years of witness.* Piedmont Press.

Lemay, T. J. (1839). *Documents on the subject of common schools published agreeably to Resolution of Legislature of North Carolina.* Thos. J. Lemay.

Lower Monthly Meeting Minutes. (1860, September 22). Maryland Hall of Records, Microfilm Number 814.

Lower Monthly Meeting Minutes. (1867, April 27). Maryland Hall of Records, Microfilm Number 814.

MacCaulay, D. (2016). Historical Quaker congregation in Suffolk commemorated with roadside marker. *Virginian-Pilot Online*. from https://www.pilotonline.com/news/article_28d69569-21c2-5c83-bf53-bf0e19445799.html.

Majors, M. A. (1893). *Noted negro women: Their triumphs and activities*. Donohue & Henneberry.

May, S. J. (1968). *Some recollections of our antislavery conflict*. Arno Press and The New York Times.

Michals, D. (Ed.), (2015). Prudence Crandall (1803 – 1890). National Woman's History Museum. Retrieved February 11, 2020, from https://www.womenshistory.org/education-resources/biographies/prudence-crandall.

Monahan, M. (1993, March 28). Hayden: Woman of Distinction Founded First Black High School. *The Tidewater News*.

Norman, E. (Ed), (2016). *African American Connecticut explored*. Wesleyan University Press.

Perdue, C., Barden, T., and Phillips, R. (Eds.), (1980). *Weevils in the wheat: interviews with Virginia ex-slaves*. Indiana University Press.

Selleck, L. B. (1994, August). *Free to cross the color line: Quaker women educators and race during the Civil War*. Quaker Lecture, Western Yearly Meeting, Plainfield, IN.

Selleck, L. B. (1995). *Gentle Invaders: Quaker women educators and racial issues during the Civil War and Reconstruction*. Friends United Press.

Strane, S. (1990). *A whole-souled woman: Prudence Crandall and the education of black women*. W.W. Norton and Company.

The Freedmen's Record (1865, December). *The Freedmen's Record, 1*.

The Friend (1883, August 1). *The Friend, 23*.

Wood, P. H. (1975). *Black majority: Negroes in Colonial South Carolina from 1670 through the Stono Rebellion*. W. W. Norton & Company, Inc.

10 | Quaker Women and Suffrage

By Jennifer M. Buck

"That it should have been necessary to form a Friends' League for Women's Suffrage seems as strange and anomalous as the formation of a Friends' Prayer League, because the purposes of both leagues would appear to be implicit in the Quaker faith" (Lunn, 1997, p.31).

Gertrude Taylor, *The Friend,* 13 February 1914

2020 marks the centennial anniversary of women being granted the right to vote in the United States. Quaker women, both as individuals and as a body, deeply shaped this movement. The intersection of Quaker values of equality, justice and that of God in all people led to an outward expression of faith that manifested itself in numerous societal issues. This essay will explore the role of Quaker women in shaping one issue in particular, the suffrage movement in the United States. Here I will highlight a few select individuals—Martha Coffin Wright, Mary Ann M'Clintock, Alice Paul, and Lucretia Mott—as well as revisit the legacy of the Seneca Falls convention itself, but only after examining some of the systemic societal forces as well as internal struggles that made the women's suffrage movement so complicated for the Quakers. This paper will primarily focus on the United States, though occasionally parallels with the British suffrage movement will be made.

Introduction

"For we have never understood how anyone brought up in Quaker traditions could be other than a supporter of women's suffrage; but we recognize. That the heroic self-sacrifice of some of those women who have gone to prison for the cause they have so much at heart must be an increased stimulus to all who believe their cause to be just." (Dandelion et al., 2019, p.73) These words from a male correspondent in 1907 speaks to the implicit Quaker assumption that equality is a shared value across genders as well as within and outside of the meeting context. Quakers understood their role to be embodying those distinctives they so claimed to believe, and to advocate unselfishly for those suffering throughout the world. Lucy Gardner, for example, leaned on that language of spiritual authority when she penned her open letter speaking to justice being served through furthering the cause of women's suffrage. In her words, "what if they [those working for women's suffrage] are the prophets and have a vision of a world redeemed by suffering and selflessness that we have not" (Dandelion et al., 2019, p.172)? During this season in Quaker history, numerous efforts were given to the cause of women's suffrage, be it through debates, letters, volunteer efforts, and even political activism in defiance of the state.

Despite their theological distinctive of equality, Quakers were not united in position or theology on the issue of women's suffrage. "Similarly, on the issue of women's suffrage there was a diversity of views among individual Quakers and within the Religion Society of Friends. If Quaker doctrine did not dictate a position on the appropriate extent of male enfranchisement, neither did it offer guidance on votes for women" (Davies & Freeman, 2004, p.99). Quakers were a body in which women had generally taken a greater public role than was common in the eighteenth and nineteenth centuries, yet there was still considerable opposition to women's emancipation and in particular, suffrage. Class can also be viewed as a factor for this, and Pamela Lunn notes that sheltered upper-class women "could not see the justice in the call for the franchise that would be obvious to them, were they working women" (Lunn, 1997, p.38). These upper middle-class women believed their place to be preserving the status quo, one dynamic only heightened by Quaker methods of corporate decision making, which tends to value consensus and moves slowly. Here in particular, women's suffrage becomes an example of Quaker parochialism. The Yearly Meeting had failed as a corporate body to understand the structural inequality it was perpetuating in failing to accept the arguments of women's suffrage campaigners, as Lunn wisely notes (Dandelion et al., 2019, p.51).

Beyond theology, not all Quaker men and women shared the same viewpoints on the issue of women's suffrage. "The great spiritual power behind the Suffrage movement is not the desire for the vote as an *asset* or a *right*, but the intense earnest longing of thousands of women for a share in the responsibility of framing the national laws, but which they, with men, are governed, and some of which at present are so hopelessly unjust to women...Friends in the past have been in the front of many a moral fight, but there is an apathy, and even intolerance on the part of many men Friends regarding the present demands of women, which is very difficult to understand..." (Dandelion et al., 2019, p.171). This editorial speaks to the gendered attitudes around the issue perceived within the Friends movement. Women's passion around the subject would be more likely to be criticized and accused of "mental instability," as Dandelion, et. al. rightly notes in their article, and both genders would appeal to passion and moral high ground to add strength to their argument (Dandelion et al., 2019, p.172). Men were not absent in this work, but overall a greater percentage of Quaker women joined the work of furthering the cause of women's suffrage.

Quakers had a movement built on the ideology of the 'spiritual equality' of women and men, both having souls. Therefore, in ministry, both had access to promptings of the Holy Spirit, both could give vocal ministry in the Meeting for Worship, both could participate in itinerant ministry and both could exercise spiritual authority. Quaker women were accustomed to speaking in gatherings and running the meetings and business affairs of the society, and thus Quaker men were accustomed to hearing women speak and lead in the polity of their religious community (Lunn, 1997). However, women's rights took a backseat to issues like peace and war, liberal social reform, or temperance. Especially after the war broke out, many Quaker women shifted their attention to war relief efforts and much of the work of the suffrage campaign became suspended. In some ways, Quaker women were never 'equal' in the Society of Friends the way that the term equality would be used today, particularly in feminist circles (Punshon, 1984). Even a term like altruism, and the idea of working towards duty and obligation of the entire society, was only beginning to become a trend around the turn of the century. Quakers were working through their understanding of the relationship between spirituality and politics, and there was a lack of agreement amongst the Society about which societal issues should be of religious concern. Sarah Bancroft Clark argued that it was precisely for the reason of standing in their testimony that they should work to change the state:

> The vote is not only a "desired privilege" but a great duty and responsibility. If Friends really understand and appreciate the value of their own great experiment in treating men and women as equals, do they not wish to share their experience with the state? Are we too comfortable to understand that the world is suffering from the lack of freedom which we possess?… May it not be possible that our inaction is the cause of the violence of which we deplore (Lunn, 1997, p.45)?

Many argued that this issue stood alongside other Quaker social testimonies such as war and slavery, stemming from the Quaker distinctive of equality. Quaker women who advocated for suffrage were known for opposing violent methods of protest, as that would have contradicted one of their other convictions of pacifism.

In Britain, this issue became hotly debated in the press as well. During the height of the movement (1906-1914), women's suffrage as a campaign ignited an entire public debate about gender roles and the use of violence in furthering social causes. In *The Friend,* a Quaker periodical, many letters appeared opposing and supporting women's suffrage. One example, from Edward Grubb, wondered "how anyone brought up in the Quaker tradition of sexual equality could be other than an avid supporter of women's suffrage" (Davies & Freeman, 2004, p.100). Another example in the press, in *The Friends' Quarterly Examiner* in 1908, Sarah Tanner proposed "if we believe in the equality of men and women in spiritual things, we can hardly deny their equality before human law, because the greater includes the less" (Lunn, 1997, p.37). A third example from *The Friend,* spoke to the "apathy" and even intolerance of men in supporting their sisters. The author writes, "the fact that for the most part Friends' homes are happy, and that the pressure of our one-sided laws seldom touches our own womanhood, should compel us to feel a greater responsibility towards the weak and ill-used among our less protected sisters" (Lunn, 1997, p.39).

Again, speaking of the British suffrage context, the evolution of the debate of the Suffrage movement in the Quaker church paralleled that in the Catholic church. The myth can be debunked that Quakers are often thought to be leaders in social change across genders where Catholics are more conservative. The Friends' Council for Women Suffrage was formed the exact same month as the Catholic Women's Suffrage Society (Lunn, 1997, p.34). Though the Quakers were not alone in being a Christian body advocating for the cause of women's suffrage, this particular cause served a pivotal role in shaping the theology of practice of the Quaker movement going forward. Dandelion, et. al. wisely speak to the value of this season in Quaker life: "Those Quakers who were passionate about the cause of women's suffrage—and who wrote of it in terms of heroism, justice, truth, self-sacrifice, prophecy, and redemptive suffering—were both laying claim to and actively creating an imminent, engaged spirituality; they were locating the divine in the mess and conflict of the real world" (p.174). From here let us examine more closely a few of the central figures in the suffrage movement as well as the lasting legacy of the Seneca Falls convention.

Mary Ann M'Clintock (1800-1884)

Mary Ann M'Clintock originated from a Quaker community in Philadelphia Pennsylvania. Through her marriage to Thomas M'Clintock they worked diligently for social reform and as Quaker ministers. In Philadelphia, she became active in the anti-slavery movement, founding the female anti-slavery society there and partnering with another abolitionist, Lucretia Mott. Her entire family migrated to western New York, settling in Waterloo in 1836, a move that became pivotal in her relationships that helped jumpstart the women's suffrage movement.

Once there, she became passionately involved in the women's suffragist movement, helping to organize the Seneca Falls Convention at her own home. Her family became involved in the Waterloo Hicksite Quaker community and her daughters, Elizabeth and Mary Ann, continued the cause of women's suffrage and went on to sign the Declaration of Sentiments. The M'Clintock family raised money for the Irish famine, the Hungarian Revolution, the abolitionist movement, and the women's suffrage cause. Their entire efforts, be in in how they ran their business, how they gave of their time, or how they opened their home, modeled the Quaker values of equality for all persons. Whether working with Frederick Douglass on the anti-slavery society chapter in their town, or co-ordinating with Elizabeth Cady Stanton to organize a women's rights convention, the passions and reach of the M'Clintock family extended far and wide. Her family home was used as a stop on the Underground Railroad and eventually became accepted into the National Park Service as an Underground Railroad Network to Freedom amongst its listing of Underground Railroad sites. The M'Clintocks continued to be actively involved in the women's rights movement they helped start throughout their life, and Mary Ann, like Lucretia Mott and others, understood the issue of women's rights as intertwined with other human rights related issues of her time.

Lucretia Mott (1793—1880)

Lucretia Mott devoted her life to the abolition of slavery, women's rights, school and prison reforms, temperance, peace, and religious tolerance. Mott became a Quaker minister, one of the only denominations allowing such a role for women, and she used her gift of preaching to speak to the Quaker distinctive of the equality of all people and the presence of the Divine light in every individual. Within the Quaker movement, she married James Mott and together the couple worked against the evil of slavery by giving speeches, founding women's abolitionist societies such as the Pennsylvania Anti-Slavery Society, and housing runaway slaves. Her own home became a stop on the Underground Railroad. Her founding of abolitionists societies was especially significant since other organizations within the antislavery movement failed to admit women. In her work for the antislavery movement, she advocated pacifism in advancing the movement based out of her Quaker convictions. She took the posture of boy-cotting any goods made or harvested by slaves, such as cotton and sugar cane, as a part of her peace testimony.

In 1837, Mott helped organize the First Anti-Slavery Convention of American Women, an event she worked on with her colleagues, the sisters Ange-lina and Sarah Grimké. This work was a part of her commitment to pacifism as well as to aid the plight of slaves toward equality for all. Another action of Mott's, which continued her controversy, was the passage of the Fugitive Slave Act in 1850. Often, facing much criticism, she connected the causes of antislav-ery and feminism. As she worked toward women's issues, Mott advocated for many issues, including equal pay for equal work as a part of her vision for both short-term and long-term reform. She served as the first president of the Amer-ican Equal Rights Association. Years after the Anti-Slavery Convention, Mott channeled her energy into the first annual women's rights convention in 1845. One byproduct of this convention was a revision to the U.S. Declaration of In-dependence titled the Declaration of Sentiments. It boldly declared, "We hold these truths to be self-evident: That all men and women are created equal," (Bar-bor & Frost, 1988, p.46) leaving in its wake a host of controversy.

Mott spoke often on the value of all people and this position led her to advocate for women's entrance into higher education, equal property rights, and the ability to vote. Her work for all the disenfranchised—women, free blacks, slaves, and Native Americans—stemmed from her deep Quaker convictions of peace and equality.

Martha Coffin Wright (1806-1875)

Mott's younger sister, Martha Coffin Wright, also significantly influ-enced the activities and organization of the first Women's Rights Convention. This Quaker family demonstrated their firm belief in equality and deep commit-ment to community through their work in social causes. Wright married Peter Pelham and after his death, David Wright. In her early years as a mother she also worked at as an educator at a Quaker school for girls. Like her sister, she ran her home as a station on the Underground Railroad, as a part of her work in the abolitionist cause alongside her good friend Harriet Tubman. She chaired several national Women's Rights conventions, and it at a visit with her sister she met with Elizabeth Cady Stanton and Jane Hunt to discuss holding a convention in nearby Seneca Falls, specifically on the topic of greater women's rights.

Wright continued to participate in the National Women's Rights Con-ventions, giving speeches around the nation and partnering in this work with Susan B. Anthony. Her daughters continued her cause of advocating for women's rights and women's suffrage, and her legacy helped found the National American Woman Suffrage Association.

Seneca Falls Convention (1848)

The Seneca Falls Convention was unquestionably shaped by Quaker women. As the first Women's Rights Convention, Seneca Falls was formed by the three women highlighted above, alongside Elizabeth Cady Stanton and Jane Hunt. These five women gathered at Hunt's home in Waterloo, New York to discuss their "long accumulating discontent" about the place of women in society. Moved by the shared sentiments, the women resolved to hold the first women's rights convention. Seneca Falls became the formalized beginning of the women's suffrage movement in America, demanding an end to legal discrimination against women (Barbor & Frost, 1988, p.355) This work came from women who were Quakers and were also closely involved in the abolition of slavery, as they saw the causes being intertwined in their goals of liberation.

For organizing the Seneca Falls convention, Mary Ann and Thomas M'Clintock planned the convention from their own home, drafting the Declaration of Sentiments in their parlor. This document, bolding declaring the equality of women and men, was read at the first Women's Rights Convention. The document went on to list eighteen "injuries and usurpations on the part of man towards woman." The M'Clintocks efforts, alongside those of other Progressive Friends, deeply affected the success of the first women's rights convention. Twenty-three Quakers signed the Declaration of Sentiments, making it the largest single group to do so. The M'Clintocks support of the convention greatly led to its success, as the couple had immense organization and public speaking experience, and their daughter Mary even served as the convention secretary, helping publish the event's proceedings. Lucretia Mott herself, also with substantive reputation, helped draw an audience as one of the speakers for the convention.

For two days, the convention comprised of six sessions primarily consisting of the role of women in society. Quaker men, like Thomas M'Clintock and James Mott, gave speeches at the convention, highlighting the gender inequality they observed in the laws of the day and chairing the public sessions through their leadership. Richard Hunt also helped the success of the convention by financing the space where the convention was held. The Wesleyan Methodist Chapel, secured through James Hunt's aid, served as one of the few venues that would be willing to host such a women's rights convention. Ultimately, drawing on the writings of another Quaker woman Sarah Grimke, the convention drafted eleven resolutions, arguing that women ought to be equal in all spheres due to their national rights. One of these resolutions, the ninth one, boldly asserted the duty of women to secure themselves the right to vote. The convention proceedings were published, and in the next two years other state and local women's rights conventions began to emerge nationwide.

Alice Paul (1885-1977)

Seventy-two years later, it was the actions and treatment of another Quaker woman – Alice Paul – which led at last to the passing of a Women's Suffrage Bill by the US Congress. Paul, building upon Susan B. Anthony's approach, took a more radical posture and demanded a constitutional amendment, after eight years of working towards her cause. The nineteenth amendment, ratified in 1920, came after years of organization building, fundraising, strategizing and campaigning on the part of Paul and her cohorts.

In 1913 on the eve of Woodrow Wilson's inaugurate, Paul organized the largest suffrage parade to date. It subsequently became attacked by a mob and hundreds of women were injured. Paul found herself arrested on charges of 'obstructing traffic,' existed in and out of prison, taking on hunger strikes to further her cause. Authorities repeatedly force-fed her, at times even forcibly admitted her into a psychiatric ward. Press coverage of this, along with continuing demonstrations, led to an outcry about prison abuse of suffragists (Cassidy, 2018). She later led protests against Wilson's failure to support women's suffrage alongside her other "Silent Sentinels," or fellow female protesters. Viewpoints on this movement shifted when the US entered the first World War in 1917, but ultimately as a result of public pressure, President Wilson called support for a women's suffrage movement a 'war measure,' reversing his earlier position. Yet it was more than just Wilson's leadership as president, for Quaker women like Alice Paul and Lucretia Mott had travelled the country for years building a coalition of support for the cause, speaking on both slavery and women's rights, and so had prepared the ground for a sea change in attitude about suffrage.

Conclusion

Many of the Quaker women who signed the Seneca Falls Declaration did not live long enough to cast their ballot. But their legacy and work continued on after their lives. The theology of the Society of Friends continued to evolve within the earth twentieth century, and Quaker theology began to align spiritual equality and temporal equality around the issue of women's suffrage. Structural critiques, such as inaction around suffrage being violent and contradicting the Quaker peace testimony, as well as their privilege and classism leading to their inaction, are valuable cautions for Quakers today as we consider what societal problems we are ignoring because of our privilege, inflicting more violence on vulnerable populations.

The work of voting equality is not yet done in this nation today, even a century after the nineteenth amendment. Mississippi became the last state in the union to ratify the amendment in 1984, proof of the difficulty of women to vote in many states for years after its passage. Issues of gerrymandering, voter suppression and restrictive voting laws keep large percentages of the United States' population from voting. Recent voting hurdles in a number of states are issues of justice and equality, as they disproportionately affect Black, Hispanic, and Native American voters and invalidate key parts of the Voting Rights Act (Liptak, 1997). The Voter Rights Act itself was an expansion and realization of the promise of the nineteenth amendment. Likewise, future legislation such as the Indian Citizenship Act, the Magnuson Act for Chinese immigrants, and the McCarran-Walter Act for Japanese Americans all serve as part of the legacy of the women's suffrage movement.

Women out-vote men. The number of female voters has exceeded the number of male voters in every presidential election since 1964. In Tina Cassidy's words,

> Imagine if every eligible woman voted. Or, at a minimum, if even another 5, 10 or 20 percent did? There is a significant gender gap in the electorate, 54 percent of which is comprised of women. A recent Quinnipiac poll found that 58 percent of women will vote Democratic in the midterms, compared with 50 percent of men; other polls show a gender gap almost twice as wide, with women favoring Democrats 15 percentage points more than men (Cassidy, 2018).

Women's suffrage continues to be needed now more than ever in the United States, and though the legality exists, the prevalence ought to continue to increase to support initiatives of equality nationwide. In order that women can expand their role and influence in society, words from 1913 still ring true today:

> In almost every nation, womanhood seeks for a fuller recognition and a larger sphere of service. It has been given to few generations to witness a movement of such surpassing importance…The history of our society brings abundant evidence of the advantage which comes to the community through a full recognition of the dignity of woman, and through according her her rightful place in family, social and church life. We as Friends, both men and women, are called to bear our share in bringing this movement to its full fruition, and in saving it from the serious dangers with which it is threatened (as cited in Lunn, 1997, p.48).

May this work of the Society of Friends continue into the 21st century, both within the United States and throughout the world.

Discussion Questions

1. What issue(s) of voting inequality do you still observe in the US today?

2. Why do you think women still vote in such low turnout, 100 years after gaining that right?

3. What movements of women's equality do you observe that echo the sentiment and spirit of the Seneca Falls convention?

References

Barbor, H., & Frost, W. (1988). The Quakers. New York: *Greenwood.*

Cassidy, T. (2018) *Men and women aren't equal—not yet. Except in the voting booth.* WBUR. https://www.wbur.org/cognoscenti/2018/11/06/imagine-a-world-where-more-women-voted-tina-cassidy.

Cassidy, T. (2019). *Mr. President, How Long Must We Wait? Alice Paul, Woodrow Wilson, and the fight for the right to vote.* 37Ink.

Dandelion, Pink, Hagglund, B., Lunn, P. and Newman E. (2009). Choose Life! Quaker metaphor and modernity. *Quaker Studies, 13*(2), 160-183.

Davies, J., & Freeman, M. (2004). A case of political philanthropy: the Rowntree family and the campaign for democratic reform. *Quaker Studies, 9*(1), 95-113.

Liptak, A. (2013). Supreme Court invalidates key part of the voting rights act," *The New York Times.* https://www.nytimes.com/2013/06/26/us/supreme-court-ruling.html.

Lunn, P. (1997). You have lost your opportunity: British Quakers and the militant phase of the women's suffrage campaign: 1906-1914. *Quaker Studies 2,* 30-56.

Punshon, J. (1984). *Portrait in grey.* Quaker Home Service.

Salitan, L., & Eve Lewis, P. (1994). *Virtuous lives: Four Quaker sisters remember family life, abolitionism, and women's suffrage.* Continuum.

www.ingramcontent.com/pod-product-compliance
Lightning Source LLC
Chambersburg PA
CBHW031301090426
42742CB00007B/546